DATA STRUCT

AND

ALGORITHMS

IN JAVA

A Comprehensive Guide

MAXWELL RIVERS

Copyright © 2023 Maxwell Rivers
All rights reserved.

INTRODUCTION

Welcome to "Data Structures and Algorithms in Java." This book is your comprehensive guide to mastering the fundamental concepts of data structures and algorithms using the Java programming language. Whether you are a beginner taking your first steps in computer science or an experienced programmer looking to deepen your understanding of the essential building blocks of software, this book is designed to cater to your needs.

Why Study Data Structures and Algorithms?

Data structures and algorithms are the backbone of computer science and software development. They are the tools that empower programmers to solve complex problems efficiently and build robust and scalable software systems. Whether you want to create cutting-edge applications, excel in technical interviews, or simply become a better programmer, a solid understanding of data structures and algorithms is indispensable.

In this book, we will go deep into a wide range of topics, from the basics of arrays and linked lists to advanced algorithms like dynamic programming and graph traversal. Each chapter is carefully crafted to provide you with a clear, intuitive understanding of the subject matter.

What This Book Offers

- **Comprehensive Coverage:** We cover a wide array of data structures and algorithms, starting with the basics and gradually progressing to more advanced topics. You'll gain a solid foundation and the knowledge to tackle real-world problems.
- **Practical Examples:** Learning is best achieved through practice. Throughout the book, you'll find numerous Java code examples that illustrate key concepts.
- **Clear Explanations:** We believe in making complex concepts accessible. We strive to provide clear and straightforward explanations, ensuring that you grasp each topic.
- **Real-World Relevance:** Data structures and algorithms are not just academic exercises; they have real-world applications. We emphasize practical scenarios, helping you understand how to apply these concepts in your projects and during technical interviews.
- **Interview Preparation:** If you're preparing for technical interviews with top tech companies, you're in the right place. We include a dedicated chapter

on interview preparation, complete with common interview questions and solutions.

Who Should Read This Book?

This book is suitable for a wide range of readers:

- **Students:** If you're pursuing a degree in computer science or a related field, this book will serve as a valuable companion to your coursework.
- **Programmers:** Experienced developers looking to enhance their knowledge of data structures and algorithms or refresh their skills will find this book beneficial.
- **Job Seekers:** If you're preparing for technical interviews, the content in this book will help you tackle algorithmic questions with confidence.
- **Enthusiasts:** Even if you're not pursuing a formal education or a career change, you can use this book to deepen your understanding of programming concepts.

Prerequisites for the Book

To make the most of this book, it's helpful to have a basic understanding of programming concepts, particularly in Java. Familiarity with the Java programming language will be an advantage, but we'll provide explanations and examples to help you grasp the language features as we go along.

By the end of this book, you'll have the knowledge and confidence to tackle complex programming challenges and excel in your software development endeavors.

CONTENTS

INTRODUCTION TO DATA STRUCTURES AND ALGORITHMS 1
   What are Data Structures? 1
   What are Algorithms? 3
   Importance of Choosing the Right Data Structure 4
   Time and Space Complexity Analysis 6

BASICS OF JAVA PROGRAMMING 9
   Setting up Java Development Environment 9
   Variables, Data Types, and Operators 11
   Control Flow (if-else, loops) 13
   Functions and Methods 15
   Exception Handling 18

ARRAYS AND STRINGS 21
   Introduction to Arrays 21
   Array Operations (Insertion, Deletion, Searching) 23
   Strings in Java 26
   String Operations 28

LINKED LISTS 31
   Singly Linked Lists 31
   Doubly Linked Lists 34
   Circular Linked Lists 36
   Linked List Operations (Insertion, Deletion, Traversal) 39
   Applications and Examples 42

STACKS AND QUEUES 45
   Introduction to Stacks 45
   Stack Operations (Push, Pop, Peek) 47
   Implementing Stacks in Java 48
   Introduction to Queues 51
   Queue Operations (Enqueue, Dequeue, Peek) 53
   Implementing Queues in Java 55
   Applications and Examples 58

TREES AND GRAPHS 60
Introduction to Trees 60
Binary Trees and Binary Search Trees 61
Tree Traversals (Inorder, Preorder, Postorder) 63
Introduction to Graphs 65
Graph Representations (Adjacency Matrix, Adjacency List) 66
Graph Traversals (BFS, DFS) 68

SORTING AND SEARCHING ALGORITHMS 71
Bubble Sort 71
Selection Sort 72
Quick Sort 73
Merge Sort 74
Binary Search 76
Linear Search 77
Performance Analysis 78

ADVANCED DATA STRUCTURES 80
Hash Tables and Hashing 80
Heaps and Priority Queues 81
Disjoint Set (Union-Find) 83
Trie Data Structure 84

ALGORITHM DESIGN TECHNIQUES 86
Greedy Algorithms 86
Divide and Conquer 87
Dynamic Programming 88
Backtracking 90
Introduction to Complexity Classes (P vs NP) 91

ADVANCED TOPICS 93
Graph Algorithms 93
Advanced Searching Techniques: KMP and Rabin-Karp 94
Computational Geometry 95
NP-Hard and NP-Complete Problems 96

JAVA LIBRARIES AND FRAMEWORKS 99

- Java Collections Framework 99
- Java Streams API 100
- Third-party Libraries for Data Structures and Algorithms: Expanding Your Toolkit 102
- BEST PRACTICES AND TIPS 104
  - Code Optimization: Enhancing Efficiency and Performance 104
  - Debugging and Testing: Ensuring Code Reliability and Quality 105
  - Handling Edge Cases 107
  - Choosing the Right Data Structure and Algorithm 108
- INTERVIEW PREPARATION 111
  - Tips For Technical Interviews 111
  - Common Interview Questions and Solutions 112

INTRODUCTION TO DATA STRUCTURES AND ALGORITHMS

What are Data Structures?

In the world of computer science and programming, data structures are the foundational constructs that allow us to organize, store, and manipulate data efficiently. Think of them as the blueprints for how data is organized and accessed within a program. Just as architects use different building materials to design and construct various structures, programmers use data structures to manage different types of data effectively.

Data structures serve as the bedrock upon which computer programs are built. They determine how data is stored in memory and how operations can be performed on that data. In essence, data structures provide a framework for managing data in a way that optimizes both time and space.

Why Data Structures Matter

The choice of data structure is not arbitrary; it profoundly influences the performance, readability, and maintainability of your code. Imagine you have a dataset containing millions of records, and you need to search for a specific item frequently. The choice of data structure can mean the difference between a search that takes milliseconds and one that takes minutes. Similarly, data structures impact memory usage, which is crucial when working with resource-constrained systems.

Here are some key reasons why understanding and using data structures is essential for any programmer:

1. **Efficiency:** Well-designed data structures can dramatically improve the efficiency of operations such as searching, inserting, and deleting data. By choosing the right data structure for a particular task, you can significantly reduce the time it takes to perform these operations.
2. **Optimized Resource Usage:** Data structures also play a vital role in managing memory and other system resources. Choosing appropriate data

structures can help minimize memory consumption and optimize resource utilization.
3. **Problem Solving:** Many programming problems can be solved more elegantly and efficiently by leveraging the appropriate data structures. Whether you're working on sorting a list of numbers or building a search engine, data structures are at the heart of your solution.
4. **Code Readability:** Using well-known data structures makes your code more understandable and maintainable. When other programmers see that you're using familiar structures like arrays, lists, or trees, they can quickly grasp the intent of your code.
5. **Interviews and Career Advancement:** In technical interviews for software development positions, a strong understanding of data structures is often a key factor in success. Many companies assess a candidate's ability to solve complex problems efficiently using data structures and algorithms.

Types of Data Structures

Data structures come in various forms, each tailored to specific use cases and scenarios. Some of the most common data structures include:

- **Arrays:** Ordered collections of elements with constant-time access to each element by index.
- **Linked Lists:** Linear data structures composed of nodes, each containing data and a reference to the next node.
- **Stacks and Queues:** Specialized linear data structures for managing elements in a Last-In-First-Out (LIFO) or First-In-First-Out (FIFO) order, respectively.
- **Trees:** Hierarchical data structures with nodes organized in a tree-like fashion, including binary trees, binary search trees, and more.
- **Graphs:** Non-linear data structures composed of nodes and edges, used for modeling complex relationships between data points.
- **Hash Tables:** Data structures that enable efficient key-value pair lookups based on a hash function.
- **Heaps:** Specialized trees for efficient priority queue operations.

These are just a few examples, and there are many more data structures available, each with its own unique strengths and use cases. As we progress through this book, we'll explore these data structures in-depth, providing you with a comprehensive understanding of how they work and when to use them.

What are Algorithms?

Algorithms are the beating heart of computer science and programming. They are the step-by-step instructions that guide a computer in solving a specific problem or performing a particular task. If data structures provide the organizational structure for data, algorithms provide the recipe for manipulating and transforming that data effectively.

In essence, algorithms are sets of well-defined rules and procedures that enable computers to solve problems systematically. Think of them as the algorithms humans use in everyday life, like following a recipe to cook a meal or following a set of instructions to assemble furniture. Similarly, computer algorithms provide a structured approach to accomplishing tasks with precision and efficiency.

The Power of Algorithms

Algorithms are the workhorses of software development, and they play a pivotal role in computer science for several reasons:

1. **Problem Solving:** Algorithms are the tools we use to tackle complex problems. They allow us to break down intricate tasks into smaller, manageable steps that a computer can execute.
2. **Efficiency:** Well-designed algorithms can significantly improve the efficiency of computations and data manipulations. They can mean the difference between a program that runs in seconds and one that takes hours or even days to complete.
3. **Reusability:** Once you've developed a well-structured algorithm for a particular problem, you can reuse it in various applications. This reusability is a hallmark of good software engineering practice.
4. **Optimization:** Algorithms can be fine-tuned and optimized to make them faster, use less memory, or adapt to specific constraints and requirements.
5. **Scalability:** As data sizes and problem complexities grow, the right algorithms ensure that your software can scale to meet those demands without a significant loss of performance.

Characteristics of Algorithms

To be effective, algorithms should possess several key characteristics:

- **Input:** Algorithms take some input, whether it's data, parameters, or variables, and process it to produce an output.

- **Well-Defined:** Algorithms must have precisely defined steps that can be followed without ambiguity. They should be deterministic, meaning that given the same input, they produce the same output every time.
- **Finiteness:** Algorithms must terminate after a finite number of steps. They should not run indefinitely.
- **Correctness:** Algorithms should produce the correct output for all valid inputs. This correctness is essential, especially in critical applications.
- **Efficiency:** Efficiency is a crucial aspect of algorithms. An efficient algorithm performs its task in the least amount of time and uses the least amount of resources possible.

Types of Algorithms

Algorithms come in various forms, each suited to specific types of problems and tasks. Some common types of algorithms include:

- **Sorting Algorithms:** Algorithms that arrange elements in a specific order, such as alphabetical or numerical.
- **Search Algorithms:** Algorithms that locate a particular item in a dataset.
- **Graph Algorithms:** Algorithms designed to traverse, analyze, and manipulate graphs.
- **Dynamic Programming Algorithms:** Techniques for solving problems by breaking them down into smaller subproblems and solving each subproblem only once.
- **Greedy Algorithms:** Algorithms that make locally optimal choices at each step with the hope of finding a global optimum.
- **Backtracking Algorithms:** Techniques for exploring all possible solutions to a problem.
- **Divide and Conquer Algorithms:** Strategies that break down a problem into smaller subproblems and solve them independently.
- **Randomized Algorithms:** Algorithms that use randomization to make decisions or achieve certain results.

Importance of Choosing the Right Data Structure

Imagine you're planning to build a magnificent skyscraper. To construct such a marvel, you wouldn't use wooden logs as the primary building material, nor would you use glass for load-bearing columns. Instead, you'd select materials like steel and concrete that are specifically engineered to handle the structural demands of such a colossal project. This decision is analogous to the importance of selecting the right data structure in programming.

In the world of software development, the choice of a data structure is akin to selecting the right building material for a construction project. It determines how efficiently your program can manage, access, and manipulate data. The right data structure can make your code efficient, readable, and maintainable, while the wrong choice can lead to sluggish performance, wasted memory, and headaches for developers.

Here are some compelling reasons why choosing the right data structure is paramount:

1. Efficiency: Different data structures excel at different operations. For instance, an array provides fast access to elements by index, while a linked list is efficient at insertions and deletions. By selecting the appropriate data structure for your specific task, you can optimize the performance of your code. Consider the impact on performance when searching for an item in a dataset of a million records using an inefficient data structure—it can be the difference between a near-instant result and a lengthy wait.

2. Memory Usage: Each data structure has its own memory requirements. Some are more memory-efficient than others. Choosing a data structure that minimizes memory usage can be crucial when working with resource-constrained systems, such as mobile devices or embedded systems.

3. Readability and Maintainability: Code that uses well-suited data structures is often more readable and easier to maintain. When other developers review your code, they can quickly understand your intent if you've chosen familiar and appropriate data structures.

4. Adaptability: Some data structures are versatile and can adapt to changing requirements. Choosing flexible data structures allows your code to evolve more gracefully as project specifications change over time.

5. Problem Solving: Many programming problems become simpler when the right data structure is used. For instance, tasks like finding the maximum value in an array or checking for duplicate elements become more straightforward with the right choice of data structure.

6. Interview Success: If you're preparing for technical interviews, proficiency in selecting and using data structures is often a key criterion for success. Interviewers frequently pose problems that require choosing the right data structure to solve efficiently.

Examples of Data Structure Selection

To illustrate the importance of data structure selection, let's consider a few examples:

1. **Text Editing Application:** In a text editing application, selecting a dynamic array (ArrayList in Java) for storing the text content allows for efficient insertions and deletions. In contrast, using a simple array would require shifting characters each time an insertion or deletion occurs, leading to poor performance.
2. **Dictionary Application:** When building a dictionary application, a hash table can provide fast word lookups. Using a linked list to store words would require a linear search, resulting in slow search times.
3. **GPS Navigation:** For a GPS navigation system, a graph data structure is invaluable for modeling road networks and finding the shortest route between two points. Using an array or a linked list would be ill-suited for such a task.

In each of these examples, the choice of data structure significantly impacts the efficiency and functionality of the software. Selecting the right data structure is akin to choosing the appropriate tool for a specific job—it can make all the difference.

Time and Space Complexity Analysis

In the world of computer science and programming, efficiency is paramount. When designing algorithms and selecting data structures, one of the central concerns is how efficiently a program will execute and how much memory it will consume. To answer these questions, we turn to time and space complexity analysis.

Time Complexity: Measuring Efficiency

Time complexity is a measure of how the execution time of an algorithm or program grows as the input size increases. In other words, it quantifies the efficiency of an algorithm in terms of time. Time complexity is expressed as a function of the input size, typically denoted as "n." It helps us answer questions like, "How does the algorithm's runtime change when we double the size of the input?"

Analyzing the time complexity of an algorithm provides insights into its efficiency and scalability. We often classify algorithms into different categories based on their time complexity. Some common classifications include:

- **Constant Time (O(1)):** Algorithms with constant time complexity have execution times that do not depend on the input size. They perform the same number of operations regardless of how large the input is.

- **Linear Time (O(n)):** Algorithms with linear time complexity have execution times that grow linearly with the input size. If doubling the input size doubles the execution time, the algorithm is said to have linear time complexity.
- **Logarithmic Time (O(log n)):** Algorithms with logarithmic time complexity have execution times that grow logarithmically with the input size. These algorithms are often highly efficient, especially for large datasets.
- **Quadratic Time (O(n^2)):** Algorithms with quadratic time complexity have execution times that grow quadratically with the input size. These algorithms can become slow for larger inputs.
- **Exponential Time (O(2^n)):** Algorithms with exponential time complexity have execution times that grow exponentially with the input size. These algorithms can become prohibitively slow for even moderately sized inputs.

Analyzing the time complexity of an algorithm allows us to make informed decisions about which algorithm to use for a given problem. It helps us balance efficiency and correctness in our software.

Space Complexity: Measuring Memory Usage

Space complexity, on the other hand, measures how much memory an algorithm or program uses as a function of the input size. It helps us understand the memory efficiency of an algorithm. Space complexity is also expressed as a function of the input size, often denoted as "n."

Just as with time complexity, we classify algorithms into different categories based on their space complexity:

- **Constant Space (O(1)):** Algorithms with constant space complexity use a fixed amount of memory that does not depend on the input size.
- **Linear Space (O(n)):** Algorithms with linear space complexity use memory that grows linearly with the input size.
- **Logarithmic Space (O(log n)):** Algorithms with logarithmic space complexity use memory that grows logarithmically with the input size.
- **Quadratic Space (O(n^2)):** Algorithms with quadratic space complexity use memory that grows quadratically with the input size.
- **Exponential Space (O(2^n)):** Algorithms with exponential space complexity use memory that grows exponentially with the input size.

Analyzing the space complexity of an algorithm is essential for ensuring that your program does not run out of memory, especially when dealing with large datasets or resource-constrained environments.

Why Complexity Analysis Matters

Time and space complexity analysis is not just a theoretical exercise—it has practical implications for software development. Understanding the complexities of algorithms and data structures allows you to:

1. **Choose the Right Algorithm:** By analyzing time and space complexity, you can select the most efficient algorithm for a given problem, ensuring that your software performs well.
2. **Optimize Existing Code:** You can identify bottlenecks in your code and make optimizations to improve its efficiency.
3. **Scale Your Software:** Efficient algorithms and data structures are crucial for scaling software to handle larger datasets and user loads.
4. **Resource Management:** Analyzing space complexity helps you manage memory effectively, reducing the risk of memory-related issues like crashes or slowdowns.
5. **Competitive Programming:** In coding competitions and technical interviews, time complexity analysis is often a decisive factor in solving problems efficiently within tight constraints.

BASICS OF JAVA PROGRAMMING

Setting up Java Development Environment

Before we dive into the world of Java programming, it's essential to ensure that you have a properly configured Java development environment. This environment consists of the necessary tools and configurations that allow you to write, compile, and run Java code seamlessly.

1. Install Java Development Kit (JDK):

The first step in setting up your Java development environment is to install the Java Development Kit (JDK). The JDK contains the Java compiler (javac) and the Java Runtime Environment (JRE), which is required to run Java applications. Follow these steps to install the JDK:

- Visit the official Oracle JDK download page or the OpenJDK website (if you prefer open-source alternatives).
- Download the appropriate JDK version for your operating system (Windows, macOS, or Linux).
- Run the installer and follow the installation instructions.

Once the JDK is installed, you can verify its installation by opening a terminal or command prompt and running the following command:

java -version

This command should display the installed Java version.

2. Set up the Java Development Environment (IDE):

While you can write Java code in a simple text editor and compile it using the command line, using an Integrated Development Environment (IDE) can significantly enhance your productivity. Some popular Java IDEs include:

- **Eclipse:** A free and open-source IDE known for its extensibility and wide adoption in the Java community.
- **IntelliJ IDEA:** A powerful commercial IDE that offers a free community edition and a paid ultimate edition with advanced features.
- **NetBeans:** Another free and open-source IDE that provides excellent support for Java development.

Choose an IDE that suits your preferences and install it on your system. These IDEs typically include built-in code editors, code debugging tools, and project management features, making your development process more efficient.

3. Configure Java Environment Variables (Optional):

Depending on your system, you may need to configure Java environment variables to ensure that your Java installation is recognized by your operating system and IDE. Here's how to do it:

- **Windows:** Go to the "System Properties" > "Advanced" > "Environment Variables." Under "System variables," find the "Path" variable and add the path to your Java installation (e.g., C:\Program Files\Java\jdk1.8.0_301\bin). This allows you to run Java commands from any command prompt.
- **macOS and Linux:** Open your shell configuration file (e.g., .bashrc, .bash_profile, or .zshrc) and add the following line to set the JAVA_HOME variable:

export JAVA_HOME=/path/to/your/java/installation

Then, add the bin directory of your Java installation to your PATH variable:

export PATH=$PATH:$JAVA_HOME/bin

Remember to replace /path/to/your/java/installation with the actual path to your Java installation directory.

4. Create Your First Java Program:

To verify that your Java development environment is correctly set up, let's create a simple "Hello, World!" program. Open your chosen IDE and follow these steps:

- Create a new Java project or file.
- Write the following Java code:

public class HelloWorld {
    public static void main(String[] args) {

        System.out.println("Hello, World!");
    }
}

- Save the file with a .java extension (e.g., HelloWorld.java).
- Compile and run the program using the IDE's built-in tools.

If everything is set up correctly, you should see "Hello, World!" displayed in your IDE's output console.

Congratulations! You've successfully set up your Java development environment. You are now ready to explore the basics of Java programming, which will form the foundation for our journey into data structures and algorithms.

Variables, Data Types, and Operators

In the world of programming, variables, data types, and operators form the foundational elements for building code. These concepts allow you to work with data, perform computations, and make your programs dynamic and responsive.

1. Variables and Data Types:

- **Variables:** In Java, a variable is a named storage location that can hold data. Variables are used to store and manage information in your programs. They have a data type, a name, and a value. For example:

]int age = 30;
String name = "John";

In this example, we declare two variables: age of type int and name of type String.

- **Data Types:** Java is a statically typed language, which means that each variable must have a declared data type. Common data types in Java include:
    - **Primitive Data Types:** These are the basic building blocks of data. Examples include int (integer), double (floating-point number), boolean (true or false), and char (single character).
    - **Reference Data Types:** These data types refer to objects or complex data structures. Examples include String (text), Arrays (collections of elements), and user-defined classes.

2. Operators:

- **Arithmetic Operators:** Arithmetic operators allow you to perform basic mathematical operations. Common arithmetic operators include + (addition), - (subtraction), * (multiplication), / (division), and % (modulo).
- **Assignment Operators:** Assignment operators are used to assign values to variables. The most basic assignment operator is =. For example:

int x = 5; // Assigns the value 5 to the variable x

- **Comparison Operators:** Comparison operators allow you to compare values. Common comparison operators include == (equal), != (not equal), < (less than), > (greater than), <= (less than or equal to), and >= (greater than or equal to).
- **Logical Operators:** Logical operators are used to perform logical operations on boolean values. Common logical operators include && (logical AND), || (logical OR), and ! (logical NOT).
- **Increment and Decrement Operators:** Java provides two special operators, ++ (increment) and -- (decrement), to easily increase or decrease the value of a variable by 1.

3. Type Casting:

- **Type Casting:** Type casting is the process of converting one data type into another. It can be explicit (done by the programmer) or implicit (done automatically by Java). For example, you can cast a double to an int to truncate the decimal part:

double price = 42.99;
int dollars = (int) price; // Explicit type casting

4. Comments:

- **Comments:** Comments in Java are used to add human-readable explanations to your code. Java supports single-line comments (starting with //) and multi-line comments (enclosed between /* and */). Comments are ignored by the compiler and are useful for documentation and clarifying code.

// This is a single-line comment

/*
This is a
multi-line comment
*/

Before we proceed, take some time to experiment with variables, data types, and operators in your Java development environment. Write small programs to practice working with different data types and performing operations. This hands-on experience will help solidify your understanding and prepare you for more advanced concepts in Java programming.

Control Flow (if-else, loops)

In Java, control flow statements are used to dictate the order of execution in your program. These statements allow you to make decisions, execute code conditionally, and create repetitive structures to perform tasks iteratively.

1. if-else Statements:

- **if Statement:** The if statement is used to make decisions in your code based on a condition. If the condition evaluates to true, the code block within the if statement is executed. Otherwise, it is skipped. For example:

```java
int age = 18;

if (age >= 18) {
    System.out.println("You are an adult.");
}
```

- **else Statement:** The else statement is used in conjunction with the if statement to specify an alternative code block to execute if the if condition is false. For example:

```java
int age = 15;

if (age >= 18) {
    System.out.println("You are an adult.");
} else {
    System.out.println("You are a minor.");
}
```

- **else if Statement:** The else if statement allows you to specify additional conditions to test if the preceding if condition is false. This construct is useful for handling multiple cases. For example:

```java
int age = 25;

if (age < 18) {
    System.out.println("You are a minor.");
```

```
} else if (age < 65) {
   System.out.println("You are an adult.");
} else {
   System.out.println("You are a senior citizen.");
}
```

2. Loops:

- **for Loop:** The for loop is used to execute a block of code repeatedly for a specified number of iterations. It consists of an initialization step, a condition, and an iteration step. For example:

```
for (int i = 1; i <= 5; i++) {
   System.out.println("Iteration " + i);
}
```

- **while Loop:** The while loop repeatedly executes a block of code as long as a specified condition is true. It does not have a predefined number of iterations. For example:

```
int count = 1;

while (count <= 5) {
   System.out.println("Iteration " + count);
   count++;
}
```

- **do-while Loop:** The do-while loop is similar to the while loop but guarantees that the block of code is executed at least once before checking the condition. For example:

```
   int count = 1;

   do {
      System.out.println("Iteration " + count);
      count++;
   } while (count <= 5);
```

- **Loop Control Statements:** Java provides loop control statements like break and continue to modify the flow of loops. break terminates the loop prematurely, while continue skips the rest of the current iteration and moves to the next one.

3. Switch Statement:

- **switch Statement:** The switch statement allows you to select one of many code blocks to execute, based on the value of an expression. It's often used when you have multiple cases to handle. For example:

int dayOfWeek = 2;

```
switch (dayOfWeek) {
   case 1:
      System.out.println("Monday");
      break;
   case 2:
      System.out.println("Tuesday");
      break;
   // Add more cases for other days
   default:
      System.out.println("Invalid day");
}
```

Control flow statements are powerful tools for making decisions and creating repetitive structures in your programs. They allow your code to respond to changing conditions and perform tasks efficiently. As you become more proficient in Java programming, you'll use these constructs to build complex and dynamic applications.

Take the time to experiment with if-else statements, loops, and the switch statement in your Java development environment. Create programs that use these constructs to solve various problems. This hands-on practice will help solidify your understanding and prepare you for more advanced programming challenges.

Functions and Methods

Functions and methods are essential building blocks that enable you to write organized, modular, and reusable code. These constructs allow you to encapsulate a set of instructions into a single unit, making your code more readable, maintainable, and efficient.

1. Functions vs. Methods:

- **Functions:** In a general sense, functions are blocks of code that perform a specific task. In Java, the term "function" is often used interchangeably with "method," although Java technically uses the term "method." Functions are usually standalone and not associated with a particular object.
- **Methods:** Methods, on the other hand, are functions that are associated with objects or classes. They are an integral part of object-oriented programming

in Java. Methods operate on the data stored within objects and define the behavior of those objects.

2. Declaring and Defining Methods:

In Java, methods are declared and defined within classes. Here's the basic structure of a method:

```
returnType methodName(parameters) {
   // Method body
   // Perform tasks here
   return result; // Optional return statement
}
```

- **returnType:** Specifies the type of data the method will return. If the method doesn't return anything, you can use the void keyword.
- **methodName:** The name you give to the method, following Java naming conventions.
- **parameters:** Any input data the method requires, enclosed in parentheses. If the method doesn't require any parameters, the parentheses remain empty.
- **Method body:** Contains the actual code that defines what the method does.
- **return statement:** If the method has a return type other than void, you must include a return statement to specify the value the method will return.

Here's an example of a simple method that calculates the sum of two numbers:

```
public int add(int num1, int num2) {
   int sum = num1 + num2;
   return sum;
}
```

3. Calling Methods:

Once you've defined a method, you can call it from other parts of your code to execute the instructions within it. Here's how you call the add method defined above:

```
int result = add(5, 3);
System.out.println("The sum is: " + result);
```

4. Method Overloading:

Java supports method overloading, which allows you to define multiple methods with the same name but different parameter lists. Overloaded methods are differentiated based on the number or types of their parameters. This is useful when you want to provide flexibility and convenience to users of your class or when you want to handle various input types.

```java
public int add(int num1, int num2) {
   return num1 + num2;
}

public double add(double num1, double num2) {
   return num1 + num2;
}
```

5. Static Methods:

In addition to instance methods, Java supports static methods that belong to a class rather than an instance of the class. You can call static methods directly on the class without creating an object. Static methods are often used for utility functions or operations that don't depend on instance-specific data.

```java
public static int multiply(int num1, int num2) {
   return num1 * num2;
}
```

6. Access Modifiers:

Methods can have access modifiers that control their visibility and accessibility from other classes. The commonly used access modifiers in Java are public, private, protected, and package-private (default). These modifiers determine which parts of your code can call the method.

7. Method Signatures:

A method's signature includes its name and parameter list but not its return type. Method signatures are used to uniquely identify methods within a class or interface.

8. Recursion:

Recursion is a programming technique where a method calls itself to solve a problem. Recursion is particularly useful for solving problems that can be broken down into smaller, similar subproblems.

9. Best Practices:

- Choose descriptive method names that convey their purpose.
- Keep methods concise and focused on a single task.

- Use comments to document your methods, especially for complex or non-obvious logic.
- Avoid deeply nested method calls, as they can make code harder to read and debug.

Exception Handling

In the world of software development, errors and unexpected situations are an inevitable part of the process. Whether it's a file that couldn't be found, a division by zero, or an out-of-memory condition, these issues can disrupt the normal flow of your program and, if left unhandled, result in crashes or incorrect behavior. This is where exception handling comes into play—a mechanism that allows you to gracefully manage and recover from such situations. In Java, exception handling is a fundamental concept that helps you write robust and reliable code.

1. What is an Exception?

An exception is an event that occurs during the execution of a program and disrupts the normal flow of instructions. Exceptions can be caused by various factors, such as incorrect user input, file not found, or attempting an illegal operation.

In Java, exceptions are represented as objects belonging to classes in the java.lang package. Each exception type corresponds to a specific error condition.

2. The try-catch Block:

The try-catch block is the foundation of exception handling in Java. It allows you to specify a section of code that might throw an exception and provides a mechanism to catch and handle the exception if it occurs.

Here's the basic structure of a try-catch block:

```java
try {
    // Code that might throw an exception
} catch (ExceptionType e) {
    // Code to handle the exception
}
```

- The try block contains the code that might throw an exception.
- The catch block is executed when an exception of type ExceptionType is thrown in the try block. You can specify different catch blocks for different exception types.

3. Handling Exceptions:

- **Catching Specific Exceptions:** You can catch specific exceptions to handle them differently. For example, to catch a FileNotFoundException, you would write:

```
try {
   // Code that might throw a FileNotFoundException
} catch (FileNotFoundException e) {
   // Handle the FileNotFoundException here
}
```

- **Handling Multiple Exceptions:** You can have multiple catch blocks to handle different exception types:

```
try {
   // Code that might throw exceptions
} catch (FileNotFoundException e) {
   // Handle FileNotFoundException
} catch (IOException e) {
   // Handle IOException
} catch (Exception e) {
   // Handle any other exception
}
```

- **Using the finally Block:** You can include a finally block after the try-catch blocks. The code in the finally block is always executed, whether an exception occurs or not. It's often used for cleanup operations.

```
try {
   // Code that might throw an exception
} catch (ExceptionType e) {
   // Handle the exception
} finally {
   // Code that always runs, e.g., cleanup
}
```

4. Throwing Exceptions:

In addition to handling exceptions, you can also throw exceptions explicitly using the throw keyword. This allows you to signal exceptional conditions in your code.

```
public void withdraw(double amount) throws InsufficientFundsException {
   if (balance < amount) {
```

```
        throw new InsufficientFundsException("Not enough balance.");
    }
    // Withdraw the amount
}
```

5. User-Defined Exceptions:

While Java provides a wide range of predefined exception classes, you can also create your own custom exceptions by extending the Exception class or one of its subclasses. This is useful for defining application-specific error conditions.

6. Best Practices:

- Catch exceptions at the appropriate level of your code. Don't catch exceptions too early if you can't handle them effectively.
- Provide meaningful error messages or log information when catching and handling exceptions. This aids in debugging and troubleshooting.
- Use the finally block for cleanup operations, such as closing files or releasing resources, to ensure proper resource management.

7. Checked vs. Unchecked Exceptions:

In Java, exceptions are categorized as checked or unchecked:

- **Checked Exceptions:** These are exceptions that must be declared in a method's signature using the throws keyword. They are typically used for anticipated exceptions that can be handled gracefully. Examples include IOException and SQLException.
- **Unchecked Exceptions:** These are exceptions that do not need to be declared in the method signature. They often represent programming errors and are subclasses of RuntimeException. Examples include NullPointerException and ArithmeticException.

Exception handling is a critical aspect of writing robust and reliable Java code. By properly handling exceptions, you can ensure that your programs gracefully recover from errors and provide a better experience for users. Whether you're working on a small project or a large-scale application, understanding and implementing exception handling is essential.

ARRAYS AND STRINGS

Introduction to Arrays

Arrays are one of the fundamental data structures in programming. They provide a convenient way to store and manage collections of data of the same type. In Java, arrays are widely used for various tasks, from organizing numbers to managing lists of items.

What is an Array?

At its core, an array is a container that can hold multiple values of the same data type under a single name. Think of it as a collection of individual storage slots, each capable of holding a single value. Each slot, or element, in an array is uniquely identified by an index, which starts from zero.

Arrays are particularly useful when you need to work with a collection of items that share a common characteristic or need to be accessed and manipulated in a systematic way.

Declaring and Creating Arrays:

In Java, you can declare and create an array using the following syntax:

dataType[] arrayName = new dataType[arraySize];

- dataType: Specifies the type of data that the array will hold. It can be a primitive data type (e.g., int, double, char) or a reference data type (e.g., String, a user-defined class).
- arrayName: Gives a name to the array variable, allowing you to reference and manipulate it in your code.
- arraySize: Specifies the number of elements the array can hold. This size is fixed when the array is created and cannot be changed later.

Here's an example of declaring and creating an array to store integers:

int[] numbers = new int[5];

In this example, we declare an integer array named numbers that can hold five integer values.

Initializing Arrays:

Once an array is created, you can initialize its elements by assigning values to them individually or using a loop. For example:

int[] numbers = new int[5];

// Individual initialization
numbers[0] = 1;
numbers[1] = 2;
numbers[2] = 3;
numbers[3] = 4;
numbers[4] = 5;

Alternatively, you can initialize an array during declaration, specifying its values within curly braces {}:

int[] numbers = {1, 2, 3, 4, 5};

Accessing Array Elements:

To access the elements of an array, you use their indices, starting from 0. For example, to retrieve the value at the third position of the numbers array:

int thirdNumber = numbers[2]; // Index 2 corresponds to the third element

Array Length:

You can determine the length (number of elements) of an array using the length property:

int arrayLength = numbers.length; // This will be 5

Iterating Over Arrays:

Arrays are commonly used in loops to perform operations on each element. You can use a for loop to iterate through the elements of an array, as follows:

for (int i = 0; i < numbers.length; i++) {

```
    // Access and work with numbers[i]
}
```

Arrays in Java are Fixed-Size:

It's important to note that once you specify the size of an array during its creation, you cannot change it. If you need to store more elements, you would need to create a new, larger array and copy the elements from the old one.

Arrays in Java are a powerful tool for organizing and managing data, but they do have limitations regarding size and flexibility. In situations where you need a dynamically resizable collection, you can explore other data structures provided by Java's Collections Framework, such as ArrayLists.

Array Operations (Insertion, Deletion, Searching)

Arrays provide a convenient way to store and manage collections of data, but their true power lies in the ability to perform various operations on the data they hold.

1. Insertion:

Inserting an element into an array involves adding a new value at a specific position within the array. To perform insertion, follow these steps:

- Determine the index at which you want to insert the new element.
- Shift the existing elements to the right, starting from the chosen index, to make room for the new element.
- Assign the new element to the chosen index.

Here's an example of inserting a value into an integer array:

```
int[] numbers = {1, 2, 3, 4, 5};
int insertIndex = 2; // Index at which to insert
int newValue = 10;

// Shift existing elements to the right
for (int i = numbers.length - 1; i > insertIndex; i--) {
    numbers[i] = numbers[i - 1];
}

// Insert the new value
numbers[insertIndex] = newValue;
```

After this operation, the numbers array will contain {1, 2, 10, 3, 4, 5}.

2. Deletion:

Deleting an element from an array involves removing a specific value from the array. To perform deletion, follow these steps:

- Determine the index of the element you want to delete.
- Shift the elements to the left, starting from the index after the deleted element, to fill the gap.
- Decrease the size of the array (optional, as arrays in Java have fixed sizes).

Here's an example of deleting a value from an integer array:

```
int[] numbers = {1, 2, 10, 3, 4, 5};
int deleteIndex = 2; // Index of the element to delete

// Shift elements to the left
for (int i = deleteIndex; i < numbers.length - 1; i++) {
    numbers[i] = numbers[i + 1];
}

// Decrease the size of the array (optional)
int newSize = numbers.length - 1;
int[] newArray = new int[newSize];
System.arraycopy(numbers, 0, newArray, 0, newSize);
numbers = newArray;
```

After this operation, the numbers array will contain {1, 2, 3, 4, 5}.

3. Searching:

Searching for an element in an array involves examining each element to find a specific value. Common searching techniques include linear search and binary search.

- **Linear Search:** In a linear search, you iterate through the elements of the array one by one until you find the desired value or reach the end of the array. It's a simple but less efficient search method for unsorted arrays.

```
int[] numbers = {1, 2, 3, 4, 5};
int target = 3; // Value to search for
boolean found = false;

for (int i = 0; i < numbers.length; i++) {
```

```java
    if (numbers[i] == target) {
       found = true;
       break;
    }
  }
}

if (found) {
   System.out.println("Element found!");
} else {
   System.out.println("Element not found.");
}
```

- **Binary Search:** Binary search is an efficient search algorithm for sorted arrays. It repeatedly divides the search interval in half, significantly reducing the number of elements to be checked.

```java
int[] numbers = {1, 2, 3, 4, 5};
int target = 3; // Value to search for
int low = 0;
int high = numbers.length - 1;
boolean found = false;

while (low <= high) {
   int mid = (low + high) / 2;

   if (numbers[mid] == target) {
      found = true;
      break;
   } else if (numbers[mid] < target) {
      low = mid + 1;
   } else {
      high = mid - 1;
   }
}

if (found) {
   System.out.println("Element found!");
} else {
   System.out.println("Element not found.");
}
```

Array operations such as insertion, deletion, and searching are fundamental to solving various programming problems efficiently. Understanding how to manipulate arrays allows you to work with collections of data effectively, making your programs more versatile and capable of handling real-world scenarios.

Strings in Java

Strings are a fundamental and widely used data type in Java and many other programming languages. They represent sequences of characters and are essential for working with textual data.

1. What is a String?

In Java, a string is an object that represents a sequence of characters. These characters can include letters, digits, symbols, and even whitespace. Strings are used to store and manipulate textual data, making them a vital part of most Java applications.

2. Creating Strings:

There are several ways to create strings in Java:

- **Using String Literals:** The most common way to create a string is by enclosing characters in double quotes:

String message = "Hello, World!";

- **Using the new Keyword:** You can also create a string using the new keyword, but this method is less common:

String message = new String("Hello, World!");

- **Using String Constructors:** Java provides several constructors for creating strings from character arrays, bytes, or other strings. For example:

char[] charArray = {'H', 'e', 'l', 'l', 'o'};
String message = new String(charArray);

3. String Operations:

Strings support a wide range of operations, allowing you to manipulate, search, and extract data from them. Here are some common string operations:

- **Concatenation:** You can concatenate (join) two strings together using the + operator:

String firstName = "John";
String lastName = "Doe";

String fullName = firstName + " " + lastName;

- **Length:** You can find the length (number of characters) of a string using the length() method:

String message = "Hello, World!";
int length = message.length(); // length will be 13

- **Substring:** To extract a portion of a string, you can use the substring() method:

String message = "Hello, World!";
String substring = message.substring(0, 5); // substring will be "Hello"

- **Search and Replace:** You can search for substrings within a string using methods like indexOf() and replace():

String message = "Hello, World!";
int index = message.indexOf("World"); // index will be 7
String replaced = message.replace("Hello", "Hi"); // replaced will be "Hi, World!"

- **Comparing Strings:** To compare strings for equality, you should use the equals() method or its case-insensitive variant equalsIgnoreCase():

String str1 = "hello";
String str2 = "Hello";
boolean isEqual = str1.equals(str2); // isEqual will be false
boolean isEqualIgnoreCase = str1.equalsIgnoreCase(str2); // isEqualIgnoreCase will be true

4. String Immutability:

One important characteristic of strings in Java is their immutability, which means that once a string is created, it cannot be changed. When you perform operations on a string, you create a new string rather than modifying the original. This immutability ensures that strings are thread-safe and can be safely shared among different parts of a program.

5. String Formatting:

Java provides various methods for formatting strings, including the printf() method, which allows you to create formatted output with placeholders:

String name = "Alice";
int age = 30;

System.out.printf("Name: %s, Age: %d%n", name, age);

6. String Building:

For situations where you need to build a string dynamically, such as in a loop, you can use the StringBuilder class. StringBuilder is mutable and more efficient than concatenating strings using the + operator, especially when dealing with large amounts of text.

```
StringBuilder builder = new StringBuilder();
builder.append("Hello");
builder.append(", ");
builder.append("World!");
String result = builder.toString(); // result will be "Hello, World!"
```

Strings are a fundamental part of Java programming, and a strong understanding of how to work with them is crucial for building robust and user-friendly applications. Whether you're processing user input, formatting output, or manipulating textual data, strings will play a central role in your Java programs.

String Operations

Strings are versatile and frequently used in programming, often requiring various operations for manipulation and analysis. In Java, you can perform a wide range of string operations to process, modify, and extract information from strings effectively.

1. Concatenation:

Concatenation is the process of combining two or more strings into a single string. In Java, you can concatenate strings using the + operator or the concat() method.

Using the + operator:

```
String firstName = "John";
String lastName = "Doe";
String fullName = firstName + " " + lastName; // "John Doe"
```

Using the concat() method:

```
String firstName = "John";
String lastName = "Doe";
String fullName = firstName.concat(" ").concat(lastName); // "John Doe"
```

2. Length:

To determine the length (number of characters) of a string, you can use the length() method:

String message = "Hello, World!";
int length = message.length(); // 13

3. Substring:

The substring() method allows you to extract a portion of a string. You specify the starting index and optionally the ending index to define the substring.

String message = "Hello, World!";
String substring = message.substring(0, 5); // "Hello"

4. Search and Replace:

You can search for substrings within a string and replace them using methods like indexOf(), lastIndexOf(), and replace():

String message = "Hello, World!";
int index = message.indexOf("World"); // 7
String replaced = message.replace("Hello", "Hi"); // "Hi, World!"

5. Splitting:

The split() method allows you to split a string into an array of substrings based on a specified delimiter:

String csvData = "John,Doe,30";
String[] parts = csvData.split(",");
// parts will be {"John", "Doe", "30"}

6. Conversion:

You can convert strings to different data types using methods like parseInt(), parseDouble(), and valueOf():

String numberStr = "123";
int number = Integer.parseInt(numberStr); // 123

7. Comparison:

To compare strings for equality, use the equals() method or its case-insensitive variant, equalsIgnoreCase():

String str1 = "hello";
String str2 = "Hello";
boolean isEqual = str1.equals(str2); // false
boolean isEqualIgnoreCase = str1.equalsIgnoreCase(str2); // true

8. Trimming:

The trim() method removes leading and trailing whitespace characters from a string:

String padded = "   Hello, World!   ";
String trimmed = padded.trim(); // "Hello, World!"

9. Case Conversion:

You can convert the case of a string using methods like toUpperCase() and toLowerCase():

String message = "Hello, World!";
String upperCase = message.toUpperCase(); // "HELLO, WORLD!"
String lowerCase = message.toLowerCase(); // "hello, world!"

10. String Building:

For dynamic string construction, especially in loops, use the StringBuilder class, which is mutable and more efficient than repeated string concatenation:

StringBuilder builder = new StringBuilder();
builder.append("Hello");
builder.append(", ");
builder.append("World!");
String result = builder.toString(); // "Hello, World!"

These string operations are essential for working with textual data in Java. They enable you to manipulate, process, and analyze strings effectively, making your code more versatile and capable of handling various text-based tasks.

LINKED LISTS

Singly Linked Lists

A singly linked list is one of the simplest yet most fundamental data structures in computer science. It is a linear collection of elements, each of which is called a "node." Unlike arrays, singly linked lists can dynamically grow or shrink in size, making them versatile for various applications.

Components of a Singly Linked List:

A singly linked list is composed of nodes, and each node has two components:

1. **Data (or Value):** This component stores the actual data or value associated with the node. It can be of any data type, such as integers, strings, or custom objects.
2. **Next Reference:** This component is a reference or link to the next node in the sequence. It points to the node that follows the current node in the list. The last node's next reference typically points to a null value to indicate the end of the list.

Creating a Singly Linked List:

In Java, you can create a singly linked list using a class that represents nodes. Here's a simple implementation:

```java
class Node {
    int data;
    Node next;

    public Node(int data) {
        this.data = data;
        this.next = null;
    }
}
```

```java
class SinglyLinkedList {
   Node head;

   public SinglyLinkedList() {
      this.head = null;
   }
}
```

In the code above, we define a Node class with an integer data field and a reference to the next node. The SinglyLinkedList class maintains a reference to the head (the first node) of the list.

Insertion in a Singly Linked List:

One of the primary operations in a singly linked list is inserting a new node. You can insert a node at the beginning, middle, or end of the list. Here's an example of inserting a node at the beginning:

```java
public void insertAtBeginning(int data) {
   Node newNode = new Node(data);
   newNode.next = head;
   head = newNode;
}
```

In this code, we create a new node, set its data, and make it point to the current head of the list. Then, we update the head to the new node.

Deletion in a Singly Linked List:

Deleting a node in a singly linked list involves updating the next references of the nodes that point to the node to be deleted. Here's an example of deleting a node with a specific value:

```java
public void deleteNode(int data) {
   if (head == null) {
      return; // List is empty
   }

   if (head.data == data) {
      head = head.next;
      return;
   }

   Node current = head;
```

```
    while (current.next != null) {
      if (current.next.data == data) {
        current.next = current.next.next;
        return;
      }
      current = current.next;
    }
  }
}
```

In this code, we check if the head node contains the value to be deleted and update the head accordingly. If not, we traverse the list while checking each node's data until we find the target node. We then update the next reference to skip the target node.

Traversing a Singly Linked List:

Traversal involves visiting each node in the list, usually from the head to the end. Here's an example of traversing and printing the elements of a singly linked list:

```
public void printList() {
  Node current = head;
  while (current != null) {
    System.out.print(current.data + " ");
    current = current.next;
  }
  System.out.println();
}
```

Advantages and Limitations:

Singly linked lists have several advantages:

- Dynamic size. They can grow or shrink as needed.
- Efficient insertions and deletions at the beginning.
- Space-efficient compared to fixed-size arrays.

However, they also have limitations:

- Inefficient for random access (you must traverse from the beginning).
- Extra memory overhead for storing next references.
- Doubly linked lists are more efficient for bidirectional traversal.

Doubly Linked Lists

A doubly linked list is a variation of the singly linked list that addresses some of its limitations. In a doubly linked list, each node contains references to both the next and the previous nodes, allowing for bidirectional traversal. This additional information enhances the capabilities of linked lists and is particularly useful in scenarios that require efficient forward and backward navigation.

Components of a Doubly Linked List:

In a doubly linked list, each node has three components:

1. **Data (or Value):** This component stores the actual data or value associated with the node, just like in a singly linked list.
2. **Next Reference:** Similar to a singly linked list, this reference points to the next node in the sequence.
3. **Previous Reference:** This reference is unique to doubly linked lists and points to the previous node in the sequence, enabling backward traversal.

Creating a Doubly Linked List:

In Java, you can create a doubly linked list using a class that represents nodes. Here's a simple implementation:

```java
class Node {
    int data;
    Node next;
    Node prev;

    public Node(int data) {
        this.data = data;
        this.next = null;
        this.prev = null;
    }
}

class DoublyLinkedList {
    Node head;

    public DoublyLinkedList() {
        this.head = null;
    }
}
```

In this code, the Node class now includes a prev reference in addition to the next reference. The DoublyLinkedList class maintains a reference to the head (the first node) of the list.

Insertion in a Doubly Linked List:

Inserting a new node in a doubly linked list is similar to insertion in a singly linked list, with the added step of updating the previous reference of the node to be inserted. Here's an example of inserting a node at the beginning:

```java
public void insertAtBeginning(int data) {
   Node newNode = new Node(data);
   newNode.next = head;
   newNode.prev = null; // Since it's the new head
   if (head != null) {
      head.prev = newNode; // Update previous reference of the current head
   }
   head = newNode;
}
```

In this code, we create a new node, set its data, and make it point to the current head of the list. We also update the previous reference of the current head to point back to the new node.

Deletion in a Doubly Linked List:

Deleting a node in a doubly linked list is similar to deletion in a singly linked list, but we need to update both the next and previous references of adjacent nodes. Here's an example of deleting a node with a specific value:

```java
public void deleteNode(int data) {
   Node current = head;

   while (current != null) {
      if (current.data == data) {
         if (current.prev != null) {
            current.prev.next = current.next;
         } else {
            head = current.next; // Update the head if deleting the first node
         }

         if (current.next != null) {
            current.next.prev = current.prev;
         }
```

```
            return;
        }
        current = current.next;
    }
}
```

In this code, we traverse the list and, when we find the target node, update the next and prev references of the adjacent nodes to skip the target node.

Advantages of Doubly Linked Lists:

Doubly linked lists offer several advantages over singly linked lists:

- Bidirectional traversal: Efficient traversal in both forward and backward directions.
- Insertions and deletions: Efficient operations at both the beginning and end of the list.
- Better suited for certain algorithms and data structures, such as doubly ended queues (Deque).

Limitations of Doubly Linked Lists:

Doubly linked lists have some additional memory overhead due to the storage of previous references. However, this trade-off is often worth it for the advantages they provide.

Doubly linked lists are a valuable data structure to understand when working with data structures and algorithms in Java. They offer enhanced traversal capabilities and are the foundation for more complex structures like Deques and certain types of caches.

Circular Linked Lists

Circular linked lists are a unique variation of linked lists where the last node's next reference points back to the first node, forming a closed loop. This circular structure offers interesting properties and applications in certain scenarios.

Structure of a Circular Linked List:

In a circular linked list, each node has two components:

1. **Data (or Value):** Similar to other linked lists, this component stores the actual data or value associated with the node.

2. **Next Reference:** This reference points to the next node in the sequence. However, unlike in traditional linked lists, the last node's next reference points back to the first node, creating a loop.

Creating a Circular Linked List:

In Java, you can create a circular linked list using a class that represents nodes. Here's a simple implementation:

```java
class Node {
   int data;
   Node next;

   public Node(int data) {
      this.data = data;
      this.next = null;
   }
}

class CircularLinkedList {
   Node head;

   public CircularLinkedList() {
      this.head = null;
   }
}
```

The Node class is similar to the one used in singly linked lists, and the CircularLinkedList class maintains a reference to the head (the first node) of the circular list.

Insertion in a Circular Linked List:

Inserting a new node in a circular linked list can be done at the beginning, middle, or end, similar to other linked lists. The key difference is that you need to ensure that the last node's next reference remains connected to the first node to maintain the circular structure. Here's an example of inserting a node at the beginning:

```java
public void insertAtBeginning(int data) {
   Node newNode = new Node(data);
   if (head == null) {
      head = newNode;
      head.next = head; // Point back to itself for circularity
   } else {
```

```java
        newNode.next = head;
        Node current = head;
        while (current.next != head) {
            current = current.next;
        }
        current.next = newNode;
        head = newNode;
    }
}
```

In this code, we create a new node and update the next references to maintain the circular structure. If the list is empty, the new node becomes the head, and its next reference points back to itself.

Deletion in a Circular Linked List:

Deleting a node in a circular linked list requires updating the next references of the nodes that point to the node to be deleted. Here's an example of deleting a node with a specific value:

```java
public void deleteNode(int data) {
    if (head == null) {
        return; // List is empty
    }

    Node current = head;
    Node previous = null;

    do {
        if (current.data == data) {
            if (previous != null) {
                previous.next = current.next;
            } else if (current.next == head) {
                head = null; // Deleting the only node in the list
            } else {
                Node lastNode = current;
                while (lastNode.next != head) {
                    lastNode = lastNode.next;
                }
                lastNode.next = current.next;
                head = current.next;
            }
            return;
        }
```

```
        previous = current;
        current = current.next;
    } while (current != head);
}
```

In this code, we traverse the circular list while keeping track of both the current and previous nodes. When we find the target node, we update the next references accordingly.

Advantages of Circular Linked Lists:

Circular linked lists offer unique properties and advantages, including:

- Seamless looping: Natural support for looping through elements continuously.
- Applications in certain algorithms, such as circular buffers and round-robin scheduling.
- Space-efficient compared to fixed-size arrays when dealing with cyclical data structures.

Limitations of Circular Linked Lists:

Circular linked lists are not suitable for all scenarios and may be less intuitive for linear data structures or when specific traversal behavior is not required.

Applications of Circular Linked Lists:

Circular linked lists find applications in scenarios where cyclical or looping behavior is required. Some examples include:

- Circular buffers in data streaming applications.
- Round-robin scheduling in operating systems for task allocation.
- Music playlist applications where songs continuously loop.

Linked List Operations (Insertion, Deletion, Traversal)

Linked lists are versatile data structures that support various operations for inserting, deleting, and traversing elements. Understanding how to perform these operations is fundamental when working with linked lists in Java.

Insertion in a Linked List:

Inserting elements into a linked list allows you to add new data at specific positions, such as the beginning, middle, or end of the list. Here are examples of insertion operations:

- **Insert at the Beginning:**

```
public void insertAtBeginning(int data) {
   Node newNode = new Node(data);
   newNode.next = head;
   head = newNode;
}
```

- **Insert at the End:**

```
public void insertAtEnd(int data) {
   Node newNode = new Node(data);
   if (head == null) {
      head = newNode;
   } else {
      Node current = head;
      while (current.next != null) {
         current = current.next;
      }
      current.next = newNode;
   }
}
```

- **Insert at a Specific Position:**

```
    public void insertAtPosition(int data, int position) {
       if (position < 0) {
          throw new IllegalArgumentException("Invalid position");
       }
       if (position == 0) {
          insertAtBeginning(data);
       } else {
          Node newNode = new Node(data);
          Node current = head;
          for (int i = 0; i < position - 1 && current != null; i++) {
             current = current.next;
          }
          if (current == null) {
             throw new IllegalArgumentException("Position exceeds the length of the list");
          }
```

```
        newNode.next = current.next;
        current.next = newNode;
    }
}
```

Deletion in a Linked List:

Deleting elements from a linked list involves updating references to remove specific nodes. Here are examples of deletion operations:

- **Delete by Value:**

```
public void deleteByValue(int data) {
    if (head == null) {
        return; // List is empty
    }
    if (head.data == data) {
        head = head.next;
        return;
    }
    Node current = head;
    while (current.next != null && current.next.data != data) {
        current = current.next;
    }
    if (current.next != null) {
        current.next = current.next.next;
    }
}
```

- **Delete at a Specific Position:**

```
    public void deleteAtPosition(int position) {
        if (position < 0) {
            throw new IllegalArgumentException("Invalid position");
        }
        if (position == 0) {
            if (head != null) {
                head = head.next;
            }
            return;
        }
        Node current = head;
        for (int i = 0; i < position - 1 && current != null; i++) {
            current = current.next;
        }
```

```
    if (current == null || current.next == null) {
        throw new IllegalArgumentException("Position exceeds the length of the
list");
    }
    current.next = current.next.next;
}
```

Traversal of a Linked List:

Traversing a linked list involves visiting each node to access or process its data. Here's an example of how to traverse and print the elements of a linked list:

```
public void printList() {
    Node current = head;
    while (current != null) {
        System.out.print(current.data + " ");
        current = current.next;
    }
    System.out.println();
}
```

Applications and Examples

Linked lists, with their dynamic and flexible structure, find applications in various domains of software development. Understanding their use cases and practical examples is essential for harnessing their power in real-world programming scenarios.

1. Dynamic Data Storage:

a. Example: Consider a to-do list application. Linked lists allow users to add, remove, and modify tasks efficiently, adapting to the changing nature of tasks over time.

2. Undo and Redo Functionality:

a. Example: In a text editor, linked lists can be used to implement undo and redo functionality. Each node represents a state of the document, allowing users to go back and forth in history.

3. Music Playlist Management:

a. Example: Music player applications use linked lists to manage playlists. Each node represents a song, and users can easily add, remove, or reorder songs within the playlist.

4. Browser History:

a. Example: Web browsers maintain a history of visited web pages using linked lists. Each node represents a web page, enabling users to navigate forward and backward through their browsing history.

5. Symbol Tables in Compilers:

a. Example: Compilers use symbol tables to store information about variables, functions, and labels in a program. Linked lists facilitate efficient symbol lookup and management.

6. Dynamic Memory Allocation:

a. Example: In programming languages like C and C++, linked lists can be used to implement dynamic memory allocation mechanisms like malloc() and free().

7. Queue Implementation:

a. Example: Linked lists can be used to implement queues, where elements are added at one end and removed from the other. Queues are widely used in algorithms and multi-threading.

8. Stack Implementation:

a. Example: Linked lists can be employed to implement stacks, where elements are added and removed from the same end. Stacks are useful in various algorithms and parsing expressions.

9. Polynomial Representation:

a. Example: In mathematics and computer algebra systems, linked lists can be used to represent and perform operations on polynomials efficiently.

10. Memory Management in Operating Systems:

a. Example: Operating systems use linked lists to manage memory allocation, tracking available and allocated memory blocks.

These examples demonstrate the versatility and practicality of linked lists in various applications, from managing data in user interfaces to optimizing memory usage in operating systems. Understanding how to implement and utilize linked lists in Java programming is invaluable for solving real-world problems efficiently.

STACKS AND QUEUES

Introduction to Stacks

A stack is a linear data structure that follows a simple principle: last-in, first-out (LIFO). Imagine a stack of books where you can only add or remove books from the top. The last book placed on the stack is the first one you can take off. This concept of stacking and unstacking items is fundamental to understanding stacks in computer science.

Key Characteristics of Stacks:

1. **LIFO Principle:** In a stack, the most recently added item is the first one to be removed.
2. **Operations:** Stacks support two primary operations:
    - **Push:** Adding an item to the top of the stack.
    - **Pop:** Removing the top item from the stack.
3. **Peek:** You can also "peek" at the top item without removing it, allowing you to inspect the element at the top of the stack.
4. **No Random Access:** Unlike arrays or linked lists, stacks do not allow for direct access to items in the middle; you can only access the top item.

Common Use Cases for Stacks:

Stacks are used in various real-world scenarios and programming tasks due to their LIFO behavior. Here are some common use cases:

1. **Expression Evaluation:** Stacks are often used to evaluate mathematical expressions. They help maintain the order of operations by tracking operators and operands.
2. **Function Calls:** In many programming languages, function calls are managed using a call stack. When a function is called, its context is pushed onto the stack, and when it returns, it's popped off the stack.
3. **Backtracking:** Stacks are valuable in backtracking algorithms. They allow you to keep track of choices and easily revert to previous states.

4. **Undo/Redo Functionality:** Stacks can be used to implement undo and redo functionality in applications like text editors.

Implementing Stacks in Java:

In Java, you can implement a stack using various data structures, such as arrays or linked lists. Here's a simple example using an array:

```java
class Stack {
   private int maxSize;
   private int top;
   private int[] stackArray;

   public Stack(int size) {
      maxSize = size;
      stackArray = new int[maxSize];
      top = -1; // Initialize the top pointer
   }

   public void push(int value) {
      if (isFull()) {
         System.out.println("Stack is full. Cannot push.");
         return;
      }
      stackArray[++top] = value;
   }

   public int pop() {
      if (isEmpty()) {
         System.out.println("Stack is empty. Cannot pop.");
         return -1; // Return an error value
      }
      return stackArray[top--];
   }

   public int peek() {
      if (isEmpty()) {
         System.out.println("Stack is empty. Cannot peek.");
         return -1; // Return an error value
      }
      return stackArray[top];
   }

   public boolean isEmpty() {
      return top == -1;
```

    }
    public boolean isFull() {
        return top == maxSize - 1;
    }
}
```

This basic implementation provides the core functionality of a stack: pushing, popping, peeking, and checking for empty or full conditions.

## Stack Operations (Push, Pop, Peek)

Understanding how to perform fundamental stack operations is essential for effectively using this data structure in Java programming.

### 1. Push Operation: Adding Items to the Stack

The push operation allows you to add an item to the top of the stack. This operation increases the size of the stack and places the new element at the top, making it the most recently added item. Here's how you can implement the push operation in Java:

```java
public void push(int value) {
    if (isFull()) {
        System.out.println("Stack is full. Cannot push.");
        return;
    }
    stackArray[++top] = value;
}
```

In this code, value is the element you want to push onto the stack. We first check if the stack is full to avoid overflow. If not, we increment the top pointer and assign the value to the appropriate position in the stack.

2. Pop Operation: Removing Items from the Stack

The pop operation allows you to remove the top item from the stack. This operation decreases the size of the stack and returns the removed element. Here's how you can implement the pop operation in Java:

```java
public int pop() {
    if (isEmpty()) {
        System.out.println("Stack is empty. Cannot pop.");
        return -1; // Return an error value
```
```

```
    }
    return stackArray[top--];
}
```

In this code, we first check if the stack is empty to avoid underflow. If not, we retrieve the element at the current top position and then decrement the top pointer to remove the item from the stack.

3. Peek Operation: Inspecting the Top Element

The peek operation allows you to inspect the top item in the stack without removing it. It's useful for checking the value of the top element without altering the stack's size. Here's how you can implement the peek operation in Java:

```
public int peek() {
    if (isEmpty()) {
        System.out.println("Stack is empty. Cannot peek.");
        return -1; // Return an error value
    }
    return stackArray[top];
}
```

In this code, we check if the stack is empty and return an error value if it is not. If the stack is not empty, we simply return the value at the top of the stack.

Implementing Stacks in Java

In Java, you can implement a stack using various underlying data structures, such as arrays or linked lists. Each approach has its advantages and trade-offs, allowing you to choose the one that best fits your specific needs.

1. Implementing a Stack Using Arrays

One of the most straightforward ways to implement a stack is by using an array to store the stack's elements. Here's a step-by-step guide to creating a stack class using an array:

```
class StackUsingArray {
    private int maxSize;
    private int top;
    private int[] stackArray;

    public StackUsingArray(int size) {
```

```java
      maxSize = size;
      stackArray = new int[maxSize];
      top = -1; // Initialize the top pointer
   }

   public void push(int value) {
      if (isFull()) {
         System.out.println("Stack is full. Cannot push.");
         return;
      }
      stackArray[++top] = value;
   }

   public int pop() {
      if (isEmpty()) {
         System.out.println("Stack is empty. Cannot pop.");
         return -1; // Return an error value
      }
      return stackArray[top--];
   }

   public int peek() {
      if (isEmpty()) {
         System.out.println("Stack is empty. Cannot peek.");
         return -1; // Return an error value
      }
      return stackArray[top];
   }

   public boolean isEmpty() {
      return top == 1;
   }

   public boolean isFull() {
      return top == maxSize - 1;
   }
}
```

In this implementation, we use an array stackArray to store the stack's elements, an integer top to keep track of the top of the stack, and an integer maxSize to define the maximum capacity of the stack. We also include methods for pushing, popping, peeking, and checking if the stack is empty or full.

2. Implementing a Stack Using Linked Lists

Another way to implement a stack in Java is by using a singly linked list. In this approach, each node of the linked list represents an element in the stack. Here's how you can create a stack using a linked list:

```java
class Node {
   int data;
   Node next;

   public Node(int data) {
      this.data = data;
      this.next = null;
   }
}

class StackUsingLinkedList {
   private Node top;

   public StackUsingLinkedList() {
      top = null;
   }

   public void push(int value) {
      Node newNode = new Node(value);
      newNode.next = top;
      top = newNode;
   }

   public int pop() {
      if (isEmpty()) {
         System.out.println("Stack is empty. Cannot pop.");
         return -1; // Return an error value
      }
      int value = top.data;
      top = top.next;
      return value;
   }

   public int peek() {
      if (isEmpty()) {
         System.out.println("Stack is empty. Cannot peek.");
         return -1; // Return an error value
      }
      return top.data;
   }
```

```java
    public boolean isEmpty() {
       return top == null;
    }
}
```

In this linked list-based implementation, the Node class represents individual elements, and the StackUsingLinkedList class maintains the top reference. The push, pop, peek, and isEmpty methods are used to perform stack operations.

Choosing the Right Implementation

The choice between array-based and linked list-based implementations depends on your specific requirements. Array-based implementations are generally more memory-efficient and provide better random access to elements. Linked list-based implementations are more flexible in terms of dynamic sizing but may have slightly higher memory overhead.

Introduction to Queues

Queues are another essential linear data structure used in computer science and software development. Unlike stacks, which follow the last-in, first-out (LIFO) principle, queues operate on the first-in, first-out (FIFO) principle. Imagine a queue of people waiting in line; the person who arrives first is the first one to be served, and the person who arrives last must wait until others are served.

Key Characteristics of Queues:

1. **FIFO Principle:** In a queue, the first element added is the first one to be removed. It maintains a strict order based on the order of insertion.
2. **Operations:** Queues support three primary operations:
    - **Enqueue:** Adding an item to the back (end) of the queue.
    - **Dequeue:** Removing and returning the front (first) item from the queue.
    - **Peek:** Inspecting the front item without removing it.
3. **No Random Access:** Similar to stacks, queues do not allow for direct access to elements in the middle; you can only access the front and back items.

Common Use Cases for Queues:

Queues find applications in scenarios where tasks or elements need to be processed in the order they are received. Here are some common use cases:

1. **Task Scheduling:** In operating systems and concurrent programming, queues are used to manage and schedule tasks for execution.
2. **Breadth-First Search (BFS):** Queues are an integral part of the BFS algorithm, which is used in graph traversal.
3. **Data Buffering:** Queues are used for data buffering in scenarios like printing queues, network data transmission, and message processing systems.
4. **Task Management in Multithreading:** In multithreaded applications, queues can safely manage the order of tasks to be executed by different threads.
5. **Print Job Queues:** In printer management systems, print jobs are placed in a queue and processed in the order they are received.

Implementing Queues in Java:

In Java, you can implement a queue using various data structures, such as arrays or linked lists. Here's a simple example of implementing a queue using an array:

```java
class Queue {
    private int maxSize;
    private int front;
    private int rear;
    private int[] queueArray;

    public Queue(int size) {
        maxSize = size;
        queueArray = new int[maxSize];
        front = 0;
        rear = -1;
    }

    public void enqueue(int value) {
        if (isFull()) {
            System.out.println("Queue is full. Cannot enqueue.");
            return;
        }
        queueArray[++rear] = value;
    }

    public int dequeue() {
        if (isEmpty()) {
            System.out.println("Queue is empty. Cannot dequeue.");
            return -1; // Return an error value
        }
        int value = queueArray[front++];
        return value;
```

```java
    }

    public int peek() {
        if (isEmpty()) {
            System.out.println("Queue is empty. Cannot peek.");
            return -1; // Return an error value
        }
        return queueArray[front];
    }

    public boolean isEmpty() {
        return front > rear;
    }

    public boolean isFull() {
        return rear == maxSize - 1;
    }
}
```

This queue implementation uses an array queueArray to store the elements, maintains front and rear pointers, and includes methods for enqueuing, dequeuing, peeking, and checking if the queue is empty or full.

Queue Operations (Enqueue, Dequeue, Peek)

Understanding how to perform essential queue operations is crucial for effectively using this data structure in Java programming.

1. Enqueue Operation: Adding Items to the Queue

The enqueue operation allows you to add an item to the back (end) of the queue. This operation increases the size of the queue and places the new element at the rear. Here's how you can implement the enqueue operation in Java:

```java
public void enqueue(int value) {
    if (isFull()) {
        System.out.println("Queue is full. Cannot enqueue.");
        return;
    }
    queueArray[++rear] = value;
}
```

In this code, value is the element you want to enqueue into the queue. We first check if the queue is full to avoid overflow. If not, we increment the rear pointer and assign the value to the appropriate position in the queue.

2. Dequeue Operation: Removing Items from the Queue

The dequeue operation allows you to remove and return the front (first) item from the queue. This operation decreases the size of the queue and shifts the front pointer to the next item. Here's how you can implement the dequeue operation in Java:

```java
public int dequeue() {
   if (isEmpty()) {
      System.out.println("Queue is empty. Cannot dequeue.");
      return -1; // Return an error value
   }
   int value = queueArray[front++];
   return value;
}
```

In this code, we first check if the queue is empty to avoid underflow. If not, we retrieve the element at the current front position, increment the front pointer, and return the item.

3. Peek Operation: Inspecting the Front Element

The peek operation allows you to inspect the front item in the queue without removing it. It's useful for checking the value of the front element without altering the queue's size. Here's how you can implement the peek operation in Java:

```java
public int peek() {
   if (isEmpty()) {
      System.out.println("Queue is empty. Cannot peek.");
      return -1; // Return an error value
   }
   return queueArray[front];
}
```

In this code, we check if the queue is empty and return an error value if it is not. If the queue is not empty, we simply return the value at the front of the queue.

Implementing Queues in Java

In Java, you can implement a queue using various underlying data structures, such as arrays or linked lists. Each approach has its advantages and trade-offs, allowing you to choose the one that best suits your specific needs.

1. Implementing a Queue Using Arrays

An array-based implementation is one of the simplest ways to create a queue in Java. Here's a step-by-step guide to creating a queue class using an array:

```java
class QueueUsingArray {
    private int maxSize;
    private int front;
    private int rear;
    private int[] queueArray;

    public QueueUsingArray(int size) {
        maxSize = size;
        queueArray = new int[maxSize];
        front = 0;
        rear = -1;
    }

    public void enqueue(int value) {
        if (isFull()) {
            System.out.println("Queue is full. Cannot enqueue.");
            return;
        }
        queueArray[++rear] = value;
    }

    public int dequeue() {
        if (isEmpty()) {
            System.out.println("Queue is empty. Cannot dequeue.");
            return -1; // Return an error value
        }
        int value = queueArray[front++];
        return value;
    }

    public int peek() {
        if (isEmpty()) {
            System.out.println("Queue is empty. Cannot peek.");
```

```
         return -1; // Return an error value
      }
      return queueArray[front];
   }

   public boolean isEmpty() {
      return front > rear;
   }

   public boolean isFull() {
      return rear == maxSize - 1;
   }
}
```

In this queue implementation, we use an array queueArray to store the queue's elements, maintain the front and rear pointers, and include methods for enqueuing, dequeuing, peeking, and checking if the queue is empty or full.

2. Implementing a Queue Using Linked Lists

A linked list-based implementation offers more flexibility when implementing a queue in Java. Here's how you can create a queue class using a singly linked list:

```
class Node {
   int data;
   Node next;

   public Node(int data) {
      this.data = data;
      this.next = null;
   }
}

class QueueUsingLinkedList {
   private Node front;
   private Node rear;

   public QueueUsingLinkedList() {
      front = null;
      rear = null;
   }

   public void enqueue(int value) {
      Node newNode = new Node(value);
```

```java
      if (isEmpty()) {
         front = newNode;
         rear = newNode;
      } else {
         rear.next = newNode;
         rear = newNode;
      }
   }

   public int dequeue() {
      if (isEmpty()) {
         System.out.println("Queue is empty. Cannot dequeue.");
         return -1; // Return an error value
      }
      int value = front.data;
      front = front.next;
      if (front == null) {
         rear = null; // Reset rear when the last element is dequeued
      }
      return value;
   }

   public int peek() {
      if (isEmpty()) {
         System.out.println("Queue is empty. Cannot peek.");
         return -1; // Return an error value
      }
      return front.data;
   }

   public boolean isEmpty() {
      return front == null;
   }
}
```

In this linked list-based queue implementation, we use the Node class to represent individual elements, and the QueueUsingLinkedList class maintains the front and rear references. The enqueue, dequeue, peek, and isEmpty methods are used to perform queue operations.

Choosing the Right Implementation

The choice between array-based and linked list-based implementations depends on your specific requirements. Array-based implementations are generally more memory-efficient and provide better random access to elements. Linked list-based implementations are more flexible in terms of dynamic sizing but may have slightly higher memory overhead.

Applications and Examples

Queues and stacks are versatile data structures with a wide range of real-world applications.

Applications of Queues:

1. **Task Scheduling:** Operating systems often use queues to manage tasks or processes. The scheduler places processes in a queue, and they are executed in a FIFO order, ensuring fairness in task execution.
2. **Breadth-First Search (BFS):** Queues are essential in graph algorithms like BFS. BFS explores nodes level by level, making use of a queue to manage the order of nodes to be visited.
3. **Print Job Queues:** In printer management systems, print jobs are placed in a queue and processed in the order they are received. This ensures that print jobs are handled fairly.
4. **Web Page Requests:** Web servers use queues to manage incoming requests from users. Requests are processed in the order they are received, ensuring that no request is left unattended.
5. **Data Buffering:** In data transmission systems and streaming applications, queues are used to buffer incoming data. This prevents data loss and ensures a smooth flow of information.

Examples of Stack Applications:

1. **Expression Evaluation:** Stacks are invaluable for evaluating mathematical expressions. They help maintain the order of operations and handle nested expressions efficiently.
2. **Function Call Management:** Programming languages use call stacks to manage function calls. When a function is called, its context is pushed onto the stack, and when it returns, it's popped off the stack.
3. **Backtracking Algorithms:** Backtracking problems, such as the "N-Queens" puzzle or solving mazes, often use stacks to keep track of choices and easily backtrack when needed.
4. **Undo/Redo Functionality:** In software applications, stacks can be employed to implement undo and redo functionality, allowing users to revert and reapply changes.

5. **Expression Conversion:** Stacks can be used to convert infix expressions (e.g., "3 + 5") into postfix or prefix notations, which are easier to evaluate.

Practical Examples:

Example 1: Breadth-First Search (BFS) in Graphs (Queue)

BFS is a popular graph traversal algorithm that systematically explores all nodes in a graph starting from a given node. It uses a queue to maintain the order of nodes to be visited. BFS is employed in various applications, including finding the shortest path in a graph and analyzing network connectivity.

Example 2: Evaluating Postfix Expressions (Stack)

Postfix notation, also known as Reverse Polish Notation (RPN), is a way to represent mathematical expressions without the need for parentheses. Stacks are used to evaluate postfix expressions efficiently. For example, given the expression "3 5 + 2 *," a stack can be used to compute the result as follows: push 3, push 5, encounter "+," pop 3 and 5, calculate 3 + 5 = 8, push 8, and so on.

These examples showcase the power and versatility of queues and stacks in various domains. Whether you're designing algorithms, managing tasks, or solving complex problems, queues and stacks are valuable tools that simplify data management and control flow.

TREES AND GRAPHS

Introduction to Trees

Trees are hierarchical data structures that play a pivotal role in computer science and data organization. Unlike linear data structures like arrays and linked lists, trees have a branching, hierarchical structure that resembles natural trees, with a root node at the top and branches extending downward. Trees are used to represent hierarchical relationships, making them a fundamental concept in data storage, algorithms, and software design.

Key Characteristics of Trees:

1. **Root Node:** Every tree has a single root node that serves as the topmost element.
2. **Nodes:** Nodes are the building blocks of a tree and contain data or values. Nodes are connected by edges to form the hierarchical structure.
3. **Parent and Child Nodes:** Nodes in a tree have parent-child relationships. The root node is the parent of all other nodes, and child nodes branch out from parent nodes.
4. **Leaf Nodes:** Leaf nodes are nodes with no children; they are the endpoints of a tree's branches.
5. **Edges:** Edges are the connections between nodes in a tree, representing relationships or paths.

Common Types of Trees:

1. **Binary Tree:** A binary tree is a tree structure where each node has at most two children: a left child and a right child.
2. **Binary Search Tree (BST):** A binary search tree is a binary tree with a specific ordering property. Nodes to the left of a parent node have values less than the parent, while nodes to the right have values greater than the parent.
3. **Balanced Trees:** Balanced trees, like AVL trees and Red-Black trees, are binary search trees with additional constraints on their structure to ensure balanced heights. This improves search and insertion performance.

Applications of Trees:

Trees have a wide range of applications across computer science and beyond:

1. **Data Retrieval:** Trees are used in databases and indexing structures to efficiently retrieve data. B-trees, for example, are employed in file systems and database systems.
2. **Hierarchical Structures:** Trees are used to represent hierarchical data, such as directory structures in file systems, organization charts, and XML or JSON data.
3. **Algorithms:** Tree traversal algorithms, like in-order, pre-order, and post-order traversals, are fundamental in searching, sorting, and expression evaluation.
4. **Artificial Intelligence:** Decision trees are used in machine learning and artificial intelligence for decision-making and classification tasks.
5. **Compiler Design:** Abstract Syntax Trees (ASTs) are used in compilers to represent the syntactic structure of source code.

Tree Terminology:

To understand trees better, it's essential to grasp the following terms:

- **Depth:** The level of a node in the tree, with the root node having a depth of 0.
- **Height:** The maximum depth of the tree, i.e., the longest path from the root to a leaf.
- **Subtree:** A subtree is a smaller tree within a larger tree, rooted at one of the nodes.
- **Siblings:** Nodes that share the same parent in a tree are called siblings.

Binary Trees and Binary Search Trees

Binary trees and binary search trees (BSTs) are two fundamental types of trees that play crucial roles in data organization and algorithm design. They are characterized by their hierarchical structure and unique properties that enable efficient data retrieval and manipulation.

Binary Trees:

A binary tree is a hierarchical data structure in which each node can have at most two children: a left child and a right child. Binary trees are used to represent hierarchical relationships, and they find applications in various domains, including computer science, mathematics, and artificial intelligence.

Key Characteristics of Binary Trees:

1. **Root Node:** A binary tree has a single root node, which serves as the topmost element.
2. **Nodes:** Nodes in a binary tree contain data or values and can have zero, one, or two children.
3. **Left and Right Child:** Each node can have a left child, a right child, both, or neither.
4. **Leaf Nodes:** Leaf nodes are nodes with no children; they are the endpoints of the tree's branches.

Binary Search Trees (BSTs):

A binary search tree (BST) is a specialized type of binary tree with an important property: the values of nodes in a BST are organized in such a way that for any given node, all nodes in its left subtree have values less than the node's value, and all nodes in its right subtree have values greater than the node's value. This property makes BSTs particularly useful for efficient searching and sorting.

Key Properties of Binary Search Trees:

1. **Left Subtree:** All values in the left subtree of a node are less than the node's value.
2. **Right Subtree:** All values in the right subtree of a node are greater than the node's value.
3. **Recursion:** The binary search property is applied recursively to all nodes in the tree, making it valid for the entire tree.

Applications of Binary Trees and BSTs:

Binary trees and BSTs have a wide range of practical applications, including:

1. **Binary Trees:**
    - Expression trees for evaluating mathematical expressions.
    - Decision trees in machine learning and decision-making processes.
    - Huffman trees for data compression algorithms.
2. **Binary Search Trees:**
    - Efficient searching and retrieval of data, making BSTs a valuable data structure in databases and dictionaries.
    - Sorting algorithms like in-order traversal of a BST can be used for sorting data.
    - Symbol tables in compilers and interpreters for quick symbol lookup.

Example of Binary Search Tree:

Let's consider a simple example of a binary search tree:

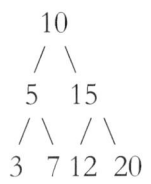

```
    10
   /  \
  5   15
 / \  / \
3  7 12 20
```

In this BST, the binary search property holds true for every node: all values in the left subtree of a node are less than the node's value, and all values in the right subtree are greater.

Tree Traversals (Inorder, Preorder, Postorder)

Tree traversal is the process of systematically visiting all nodes in a tree data structure. It's a fundamental operation for analyzing and manipulating trees, including binary trees and binary search trees. Tree traversals follow a specific order when visiting nodes, and three common traversal orders are widely used: inorder, preorder, and postorder. These traversal techniques are essential for various applications in computer science and software development.

Inorder Traversal:

In an inorder traversal, nodes are visited in the following order:

1. Visit the left subtree.
2. Visit the current node.
3. Visit the right subtree.

In simpler terms, an inorder traversal explores a binary tree from its leftmost (smallest) node to its rightmost (largest) node, producing a sorted output for a binary search tree.

Preorder Traversal:

In a preorder traversal, nodes are visited in the following order:

1. Visit the current node.
2. Visit the left subtree.
3. Visit the right subtree.

Preorder traversal is often used for constructing a copy of the tree or for printing the structure of a tree before any other operation.

Postorder Traversal:

In a postorder traversal, nodes are visited in the following order:

1. Visit the left subtree.
2. Visit the right subtree.
3. Visit the current node.

Postorder traversal is commonly used for tasks like deleting nodes or evaluating mathematical expressions represented by a tree.

Example Tree and Traversals:

Let's consider a simple binary tree for illustration:

```
    10
   /  \
  5    15
 / \  / \
3  7 12 20
```

Inorder Traversal: (3, 5, 7, 10, 12, 15, 20)

Preorder Traversal: (10, 5, 3, 7, 15, 12, 20)

Postorder Traversal: (3, 7, 5, 12, 20, 15, 10)

Applications of Tree Traversals:

1. **Searching:** Inorder traversal of a binary search tree yields elements in sorted order, making it useful for searching specific values.
2. **Expression Evaluation:** Preorder or postorder traversals are used to evaluate mathematical expressions represented as expression trees.
3. **Tree Construction:** Preorder traversal can be used to construct a tree from its serialized form.
4. **Deleting Nodes:** Postorder traversal is commonly used when deleting nodes from a tree.

Choosing the Right Traversal:

The choice of traversal order depends on the specific problem you are solving and the desired outcome. Each traversal order has its unique advantages and use cases. Understanding the problem requirements is key to selecting the appropriate traversal technique.

Introduction to Graphs

Graphs are versatile and powerful data structures that model relationships between objects. They provide a flexible way to represent not only physical connections like networks and maps but also abstract relationships such as social networks, dependencies, and more. Graphs are an essential concept in computer science and mathematics, with applications spanning from data analysis to routing algorithms.

Key Characteristics of Graphs:

1. **Vertices (Nodes):** A graph is composed of vertices (also known as nodes) that represent entities or points of interest.
2. **Edges:** Edges are connections between vertices in a graph. They represent relationships or interactions between entities. Edges can have weights or labels to convey additional information.
3. **Directed vs. Undirected Graphs:** In a directed graph (also called a digraph), edges have a direction, meaning they go from one vertex to another. In an undirected graph, edges have no direction, and connections are bidirectional.
4. **Cyclic vs. Acyclic Graphs:** A graph is cyclic if there is at least one cycle (a path that starts and ends at the same vertex). If a graph has no cycles, it is called acyclic.

Types of Graphs:

1. **Connected vs. Disconnected Graphs:** A connected graph has a path between every pair of vertices. A disconnected graph consists of two or more separate components.
2. **Weighted vs. Unweighted Graphs:** In a weighted graph, each edge has a weight or cost associated with it. Unweighted graphs have no edge weights.
3. **Sparse vs. Dense Graphs:** A graph is considered sparse if it has relatively few edges compared to the maximum possible edges. Conversely, it is dense if it has many edges.
4. **Bipartite Graphs:** Bipartite graphs have their vertices divided into two disjoint sets, with edges only connecting vertices from different sets.

Applications of Graphs:

Graphs have a wide range of applications, including:

1. **Social Networks:** Modeling connections between individuals in social media platforms.
2. **Transportation Networks:** Representing road networks, flight routes, and public transportation systems.
3. **Recommendation Systems:** Analyzing user-item interactions to provide personalized recommendations.
4. **Web Page Ranking:** Determining the importance of web pages using algorithms like PageRank.
5. **Dependency Resolution:** Managing software dependencies in package management systems.
6. **Shortest Path Algorithms:** Finding the shortest path between locations, essential for GPS and navigation systems.

Example Graph:

Consider a simple undirected graph representing social connections between individuals:

```
A --- B
| / |
C --- D
```

In this graph, vertices A, B, C, and D represent individuals, and edges represent friendships or connections between them.

Graph Representations (Adjacency Matrix, Adjacency List)

Graphs can be represented in different ways, depending on the specific application and the operations you need to perform on them. Two common representations are the adjacency matrix and the adjacency list. Each has its own strengths and is suitable for different scenarios.

Adjacency Matrix:

An adjacency matrix is a 2D array that represents a graph G with vertices V. In an adjacency matrix, the rows and columns correspond to vertices, and each cell (i, j) contains information about the edge between vertex i and vertex j. The matrix is typically symmetric for undirected graphs, while for directed graphs, it may not be symmetric.

Key Characteristics of Adjacency Matrices:

1. **Space Complexity:** The space complexity of an adjacency matrix is $O(V^2)$, where V is the number of vertices. This makes it less suitable for sparse graphs with many vertices and relatively few edges.
2. **Edge Existence:** To determine whether there is an edge between two vertices i and j, you can simply check the value of matrix[i][j]. If it's non-zero, an edge exists; otherwise, there's no edge.
3. **Edge Weight:** If the graph is weighted, the values in the matrix can represent edge weights.

Adjacency List:

An adjacency list is a data structure that represents a graph by associating each vertex with a list of its neighboring vertices. In an undirected graph, each edge is represented twice (once for each adjacent vertex), while in a directed graph, each edge is represented once.

Key Characteristics of Adjacency Lists:

1. **Space Complexity:** The space complexity of an adjacency list is $O(V + E)$, where V is the number of vertices and E is the number of edges. This makes it more memory-efficient for sparse graphs.
2. **Edge Existence:** To determine whether there is an edge between two vertices i and j, you can search the adjacency list of vertex i for vertex j. This operation typically takes $O(degree(i))$ time, where degree(i) is the number of neighbors of vertex i.
3. **Edge Weight:** If the graph is weighted, each entry in the adjacency list can store both the neighbor vertex and the edge weight.

Choosing the Right Representation:

The choice between adjacency matrices and adjacency lists depends on the specific use case:

- **Adjacency Matrix:** Use when memory is not a concern, and you need constant-time edge existence checks or when dealing with dense graphs.
- **Adjacency List:** Use when memory efficiency is essential, and you need to perform operations like traversals or edge existence checks efficiently, especially for sparse graphs.

Example:

Consider a simple undirected graph:

```
A -- B
|    |
C -- D
```

Adjacency Matrix:

```
  A B C D
A 0 1 1 0
B 1 0 0 1
C 1 0 0 1
D 0 1 1 0
```

Adjacency List:

A -> [B, C]
B -> [A, D]
C -> [A, D]
D -> [B, C]

Graph Traversals (BFS, DFS)

Graph traversal is the process of systematically visiting all the vertices and edges of a graph. Two common methods for graph traversal are Breadth-First Search (BFS) and Depth-First Search (DFS). These techniques help us analyze graphs, making them essential tools in various computer science applications.

Breadth-First Search (BFS):

Breadth-First Search is a systematic exploration of a graph that begins at a chosen starting vertex and visits all its neighbors before moving on to their neighbors. BFS is often likened to the spreading of waves or ripples in a pond, where each wave represents a level of traversal.

Key Characteristics of BFS:

1. **Queue-Based:** BFS is implemented using a queue data structure. The starting vertex is enqueued, and its neighbors are explored in a breadth-first manner.
2. **Shortest Paths:** When applied to unweighted graphs, BFS can find the shortest path between two vertices.

3. **Level Order:** BFS naturally traverses the graph level by level, making it suitable for tasks that require a layered exploration of the graph.

Depth-First Search (DFS):

Depth-First Search is a traversal technique that explores as far down a branch as possible before backtracking. It is akin to a journey into the depths of a maze, where you explore one path completely before returning to explore another.

Key Characteristics of DFS:

1. **Stack-Based:** DFS is implemented using a stack or a recursive function call stack. The starting vertex is pushed onto the stack, and exploration continues until a leaf node is reached.
2. **Recursive Nature:** DFS can be implemented recursively, making it an elegant and intuitive choice for certain applications.
3. **Path Discovery:** DFS is often used to discover paths and cycles in a graph.

Choosing Between BFS and DFS:

The choice between BFS and DFS depends on the specific problem and the desired outcome:

- **BFS:** Use when you need to find the shortest path between two vertices, explore neighbors level by level, or identify the minimum number of edges required to reach a target vertex.
- **DFS:** Use when you want to explore deep into a branch, perform topological sorting, identify connected components, or find paths and cycles in the graph.

Example:

Consider a simple undirected graph:

```
A -- B -- C
|    |    |
D -- E -- F
```

BFS (Starting from A): A -> B -> D -> E -> C -> F

DFS (Starting from A): A -> B -> E -> F -> C -> D

Applications of BFS and DFS:

- **BFS:** Shortest path finding, network routing, web crawling, and level order traversal in trees.
- **DFS:** Topological sorting, cycle detection, maze solving, and connectivity analysis.

SORTING AND SEARCHING ALGORITHMS

Bubble Sort

Bubble Sort is one of the simplest and most straightforward sorting algorithms in computer science. While it may not be the most efficient for large datasets, understanding Bubble Sort is a fundamental step in learning about sorting algorithms. Its concept is easy to grasp, making it an excellent starting point for studying sorting techniques.

How Bubble Sort Works:

Bubble Sort works by repeatedly stepping through the list to be sorted, comparing adjacent elements, and swapping them if they are in the wrong order. The pass through the list is repeated until no swaps are needed, indicating that the list is sorted.

Here's a step-by-step breakdown of how Bubble Sort operates:

1. Start with the first element (index 0) and compare it with the next element (index 1).
2. If the first element is greater than the second element, swap them.
3. Move to the next pair of elements (index 1 and index 2) and repeat the comparison and swap if necessary.
4. Continue this process, moving one step at a time, until the largest element "bubbles up" to the end of the list.
5. Repeat the process for the remaining unsorted portion of the list, excluding the last (already sorted) element.
6. Continue these steps until the entire list is sorted.

Visualizing Bubble Sort:

Consider the following unsorted list: [5, 2, 9, 1, 5, 6].

1. First pass: [2, 5, 1, 5, 6, 9]
2. Second pass: [2, 1, 5, 5, 6, 9]

3. Third pass: [1, 2, 5, 5, 6, 9]

The list is now sorted. Notice how the largest element "bubbles up" to the end of the list in each pass.

Time Complexity:

Bubble Sort has a time complexity of $O(n^2)$ in the worst and average cases, where n is the number of elements in the list. This makes it inefficient for sorting large datasets. However, for small lists or nearly sorted lists, it can perform reasonably well.

When to Use Bubble Sort:

Bubble Sort is primarily used for educational purposes and is rarely used in practical applications due to its poor performance on larger datasets. There are more efficient sorting algorithms like Quick Sort, Merge Sort, and Heap Sort that are better suited for real-world scenarios.

Selection Sort

Selection Sort is a straightforward and intuitive sorting algorithm that works by repeatedly selecting the minimum (or maximum) element from an unsorted portion of the list and moving it to its correct position in the sorted portion. Although not the most efficient sorting algorithm, it is easy to understand and implement, making it a valuable learning tool for understanding sorting concepts.

How Selection Sort Works:

Selection Sort operates in the following manner:

1. Divide the list into two parts: the sorted portion and the unsorted portion.
2. Initially, the sorted portion is empty, and the entire list is unsorted.
3. Find the minimum (or maximum) element in the unsorted portion of the list.
4. Swap the minimum (or maximum) element with the first element in the unsorted portion, effectively extending the sorted portion.
5. Repeat steps 3 and 4 for the remaining unsorted portion of the list until the entire list is sorted.

Here's a step-by-step breakdown of Selection Sort:

Consider the list: [5, 2, 9, 1, 5, 6].

1. First pass: [1, 2, 9, 5, 5, 6]
2. Second pass: [1, 2, 9, 5, 5, 6]
3. Third pass: [1, 2, 5, 9, 5, 6]
4. Fourth pass: [1, 2, 5, 5, 9, 6]
5. Fifth pass: [1, 2, 5, 5, 6, 9]

The list is now sorted.

Visualizing Selection Sort:

Selection Sort works by selecting the smallest element from the unsorted portion and swapping it with the first element of the unsorted portion. This process continues until the entire list is sorted.

Time Complexity:

Selection Sort has a time complexity of $O(n^2)$ in the worst, average, and best cases, where n is the number of elements in the list. It makes roughly $n^2/2$ comparisons and n swaps in the worst case, which is not suitable for large datasets.

When to Use Selection Sort:

Selection Sort is primarily used for educational purposes and for sorting very small lists where its simplicity outweighs its inefficiency. In practice, more efficient sorting algorithms like Quick Sort, Merge Sort, and Heap Sort are preferred for larger datasets.

Quick Sort

Quick Sort is a highly efficient and widely used sorting algorithm known for its speed and effectiveness. It falls under the category of comparison-based sorting algorithms and is often the preferred choice for sorting large datasets. Quick Sort is also a fundamental algorithm used in various computer science applications.

How Quick Sort Works:

Quick Sort follows a divide-and-conquer strategy to sort a list of elements. The basic idea is to select a pivot element from the list and partition the other elements into two sub-arrays, according to whether they are less than or greater than the pivot. The sub-arrays are then recursively sorted.

Here's a step-by-step breakdown of how Quick Sort operates:

1. Choose a pivot element from the list. The choice of the pivot can significantly affect the algorithm's performance.
2. Partition the list into two sub-arrays: elements less than the pivot and elements greater than the pivot.
3. Recursively apply Quick Sort to the sub-arrays.
4. Combine the sorted sub-arrays and the pivot to produce the final sorted list.

Visualizing Quick Sort:

Consider the list: [5, 2, 9, 1, 5, 6].

1. Choose a pivot, e.g., 5.
2. Partition the list: [2, 1] | [5] | [9, 5, 6].
3. Recursively apply Quick Sort to the sub-arrays.
4. Combine the sorted sub-arrays and the pivot: [1, 2, 5, 5, 6, 9].

The list is now sorted.

Time Complexity:

Quick Sort has an average-case time complexity of $O(n \log n)$, where n is the number of elements in the list. In the worst case, it can degrade to $O(n^2)$, but this is rare and can be mitigated with careful pivot selection strategies. Its average-case performance makes it one of the fastest sorting algorithms available.

When to Use Quick Sort:

Quick Sort is an excellent choice for sorting large datasets efficiently. It outperforms many other sorting algorithms and is often used as the default sorting algorithm in programming languages and libraries. Its efficiency makes it suitable for a wide range of applications, from database management to algorithm design.

Merge Sort

Merge Sort is a highly efficient, stable, and comparison-based sorting algorithm known for its consistent performance and reliability. It is a classic example of a divide-and-conquer sorting technique that is suitable for sorting large datasets. Merge Sort is also widely used in computer science and various applications.

How Merge Sort Works:

Merge Sort operates on the principle of dividing the unsorted list into smaller sub-lists, sorting these sub-lists, and then merging them to produce a sorted list. The core steps of Merge Sort are as follows:

1. Divide: Divide the unsorted list into two equal halves (or nearly equal if the list has an odd number of elements).
2. Conquer: Recursively sort both halves using Merge Sort.
3. Merge: Merge the two sorted sub-arrays to produce a single sorted list.

The merging process in Merge Sort is a key operation that combines two sorted sub-arrays into a single sorted array. It compares elements from both sub-arrays and places them in the correct order in the merged array.

Visualizing Merge Sort:

Consider the list: [5, 2, 9, 1, 5, 6].

1. Divide the list into two halves: [5, 2, 9] and [1, 5, 6].
2. Recursively sort both halves.

   Sort [5, 2, 9]:

   - Divide into [5] and [2, 9].
   - Sort [2, 9]: [2, 9]
   - Merge [5] and [2, 9]: [2, 5, 9]

   Sort [1, 5, 6]:

   - Divide into [1] and [5, 6].
   - Sort [5, 6]: [5, 6]
   - Merge [1] and [5, 6]: [1, 5, 6]

3. Merge the two sorted sub-arrays [2, 5, 9] and [1, 5, 6] to obtain the final sorted list: [1, 2, 5, 5, 6, 9].

Time Complexity:

Merge Sort has a consistent time complexity of O(n log n) in all cases, where n is the number of elements in the list. It guarantees efficient sorting even for large datasets. The divide-and-conquer nature of the algorithm ensures its reliable performance.

When to Use Merge Sort:

Merge Sort is an excellent choice for sorting large datasets or when stable sorting is required. It is often used in scenarios where consistent and efficient sorting is crucial, such as file sorting, database sorting, and external sorting.

Binary Search

Binary Search is a powerful searching algorithm known for its speed and efficiency. It is particularly well-suited for searching in sorted lists or arrays, making it an essential tool for finding specific elements in large datasets. Binary Search is a fundamental concept in computer science and is widely used in various applications.

How Binary Search Works:

Binary Search operates by repeatedly dividing a sorted list into two equal halves and then narrowing down the search range based on comparisons with a target element. Here are the core steps of Binary Search:

1. Begin with the entire sorted list.
2. Determine the middle element of the current range.
3. Compare the middle element with the target element.
4. If they match, the search is successful.
5. If the middle element is greater than the target element, narrow the search to the left half of the current range and repeat the process.
6. If the middle element is less than the target element, narrow the search to the right half of the current range and repeat the process.
7. Continue this process until the target element is found or the search range is empty.

Visualizing Binary Search:

Consider the sorted list: [1, 2, 5, 5, 6, 9].

Searching for the target element 5:

1. Initial search range: [1, 2, 5, 5, 6, 9].
2. Middle element: 5 (matches the target).
3. Search successful; the target element 5 is found.

Binary Search efficiently locates the target element with just a few comparisons, even in a large dataset.

Time Complexity:

Binary Search has a time complexity of O(log n), where n is the number of elements in the sorted list. This logarithmic time complexity means that Binary Search can efficiently handle large datasets, as the number of comparisons required grows slowly.

When to Use Binary Search:

Binary Search is an ideal choice when searching for specific elements in sorted lists or arrays. It excels in scenarios where quick and efficient retrieval of data is essential, such as in databases, information retrieval systems, and search engines.

Linear Search

Linear Search, also known as Sequential Search, is one of the simplest and most basic searching algorithms in computer science. It is straightforward to understand and implement, making it a valuable tool for searching for specific elements in a list or array. While it may not be the fastest algorithm for large datasets, Linear Search is a fundamental concept and serves as a foundation for more advanced searching techniques.

How Linear Search Works:

Linear Search operates by iterating through each element in the list one by one, comparing each element with the target element until a match is found or the end of the list is reached. Here are the core steps of Linear Search:

1. Start at the beginning of the list.
2. Compare the first element with the target element.
3. If they match, the search is successful, and the position of the element is returned.
4. If they do not match, move to the next element in the list and repeat the comparison.
5. Continue this process until a match is found or the end of the list is reached.

Visualizing Linear Search:

Consider the list: [1, 2, 5, 5, 6, 9].

Searching for the target element 5:

1. Start at the first element: 1 (not a match).
2. Move to the next element: 2 (not a match).
3. Continue to the next element: 5 (match found).

4. Search successful; the target element 5 is found at position 2 (0-based index).

Linear Search efficiently finds the target element by sequentially examining each element in the list.

Time Complexity:

Linear Search has a time complexity of $O(n)$, where n is the number of elements in the list. In the worst-case scenario, Linear Search may have to examine every element in the list. Therefore, it is less efficient than some other searching algorithms for large datasets.

When to Use Linear Search:

Linear Search is most suitable for small datasets or unsorted lists where the order of elements does not matter. It is a straightforward and intuitive algorithm and can be useful in various situations where simplicity is more important than speed.

Performance Analysis

Performance analysis is a crucial aspect of designing and implementing algorithms and data structures. It involves measuring and assessing various aspects of an algorithm's or data structure's performance, such as execution time, memory usage, and scalability. Through performance analysis, developers can make informed decisions about the suitability of an algorithm or data structure for a particular task and optimize their code for efficiency.

Why Performance Analysis Matters:

Performance analysis serves several vital purposes in computer science and software development:

1. **Algorithm Selection:** It helps in choosing the most appropriate algorithm or data structure for a specific problem based on factors like input size and expected workload.
2. **Optimization:** Performance analysis identifies bottlenecks and areas for improvement in existing code, allowing developers to optimize algorithms and data structures for better efficiency.
3. **Resource Management:** It ensures efficient utilization of system resources, such as memory and CPU, which is critical for software running on resource-constrained devices.

4. **Scalability:** Performance analysis assesses how well an algorithm or data structure can handle growing datasets and increasing workloads, a crucial consideration for modern software applications.

Metrics for Performance Analysis:

When analyzing the performance of algorithms and data structures, several key metrics are commonly used:

1. **Time Complexity:** Time complexity expresses how the running time of an algorithm or data structure grows as a function of the input size. It is often represented using Big O notation (e.g., O(n), O(log n)).
2. **Space Complexity:** Space complexity measures the amount of memory or storage required by an algorithm or data structure in relation to the input size.
3. **Execution Time:** Actual execution time is the elapsed time taken by an algorithm or operation to complete. It is typically measured in milliseconds or seconds.
4. **Memory Usage:** Memory usage quantifies the amount of memory consumed by an algorithm or data structure during execution.
5. **Scalability:** Scalability assesses how well an algorithm or data structure performs as the input size or workload increases. It often involves benchmarking and stress testing.

Tools and Techniques for Performance Analysis:

Performing performance analysis often involves the following tools and techniques:

1. **Profiling:** Profiling tools help identify performance bottlenecks in code by tracking function call frequencies and execution times.
2. **Benchmarking:** Benchmarking involves running a set of predefined tests to measure the performance of an algorithm or data structure under specific conditions.
3. **Instrumentation:** Instrumentation involves adding code to an application to collect performance-related data, such as execution times and memory usage.
4. **Big O Analysis:** Analyzing the algorithm's time and space complexity using Big O notation provides a theoretical understanding of its performance characteristics.
5. **Real-world Testing:** Conducting real-world tests and simulations can provide insights into how an algorithm or data structure performs under actual usage scenarios.

ADVANCED DATA STRUCTURES

Hash Tables and Hashing

Hash tables are one of the most versatile and widely used data structures in computer science. They provide a fast and efficient way to store and retrieve data by mapping keys to values through a process called hashing.

Understanding Hash Tables:

A hash table, also known as a hash map, is a data structure that stores key-value pairs. It leverages a hash function to compute an index or address for each key, allowing for quick access to the associated value. Hash tables are designed for speed, making them ideal for tasks that involve searching, inserting, and deleting data.

The Role of Hashing:

At the heart of every hash table lies the concept of hashing. Hashing is the process of taking an input (or 'key') and transforming it into a fixed-size string of characters, often referred to as a hash code or hash value. This hash code serves as an index to locate the corresponding value within the table.

Hash Functions:

Hashing relies on specialized functions called hash functions. These functions take a key as input and produce a hash code as output. A good hash function has several crucial properties:

1. **Deterministic:** Given the same input, it always produces the same hash code.
2. **Efficient:** It should be computationally efficient to compute the hash code.
3. **Uniform Distribution:** It should distribute hash codes uniformly across the table to minimize collisions (two keys mapping to the same index).
4. **Avalanche Effect:** A small change in the input should result in a significantly different hash code.

Handling Collisions:

Collisions occur when two distinct keys produce the same hash code, mapping to the same index in the hash table. Handling collisions is a crucial aspect of hash table design. Common collision resolution techniques include:

1. **Separate Chaining:** Each index in the table contains a linked list or another data structure to store multiple key-value pairs with the same hash code.
2. **Open Addressing:** When a collision occurs, this method involves probing the table to find the next available slot.

Applications of Hash Tables:

Hash tables have a wide range of applications in various fields, including:

- **Databases:** Hash tables are used for indexing and quick retrieval of records.
- **Caches:** They are essential for caching frequently accessed data to reduce latency.
- **Distributed Systems:** Hash tables are used to distribute data evenly across multiple servers.
- **Symbol Tables:** Compilers and interpreters use hash tables to manage identifiers and their associated values.
- **Password Storage:** Hashing is used to securely store and verify passwords.

Performance and Efficiency:

Hash tables offer an average-case time complexity of $O(1)$ for key-value retrieval, insertion, and deletion, making them incredibly efficient for most practical purposes. However, the efficiency depends on a well-designed hash function, collision resolution strategy, and a properly sized table.

Heaps and Priority Queues

Heaps and priority queues are essential data structures designed to manage and retrieve elements based on their priorities. These versatile structures find applications in various domains where prioritization plays a critical role, such as scheduling tasks, optimizing algorithms, and network routing.

Understanding Heaps:

A heap is a specialized tree-based data structure that satisfies the heap property. The heap property dictates the order of elements within the heap: in a min-heap, the parent node's value is smaller than or equal to its children, whereas in a max-heap, the parent node's value is larger than or equal to its children.

Priority Queues:

A priority queue is an abstract data type that extends the concept of a queue. Instead of following the traditional first-in-first-out (FIFO) order, priority queues serve elements in order of their priority. Elements with higher priorities are dequeued before those with lower priorities.

Heap Operations:

Heaps support fundamental operations like insertion and extraction of elements efficiently. The two primary operations for heaps are:

1. **Insertion:** Adding an element while preserving the heap property. This typically involves inserting the new element at the bottom of the heap and then "bubbling up" or "sifting up" the element to its correct position.
2. **Extraction (Dequeue):** Removing and returning the element with the highest (in max-heap) or lowest (in min-heap) priority. After removal, the last element replaces the root, and it is then "bubbled down" or "sifted down" to maintain the heap property.

Types of Heaps:

- **Min-Heap:** In a min-heap, the smallest element is always at the root, making it suitable for finding the minimum element quickly. Min-heaps are commonly used in tasks like Dijkstra's algorithm for finding the shortest path.
- **Max-Heap:** Conversely, in a max-heap, the largest element resides at the root. Max-heaps find applications in algorithms like heap sort, which efficiently sorts a list.

Applications of Priority Queues:

Priority queues are crucial in a variety of real-world scenarios:

- **Task Scheduling:** Operating systems use priority queues to manage tasks with different priorities.
- **Network Routing:** Priority queues help optimize routing decisions in computer networks.
- **Dijkstra's Algorithm:** This algorithm, used in pathfinding, relies on min-heaps to find the shortest path in weighted graphs.

- **Job Scheduling:** Priority queues are employed in scheduling jobs with varying priorities in batch processing systems.

Performance Analysis:

Heaps and priority queues offer efficient average-case time complexities for insertion and extraction: O(log n) for both operations, where n is the number of elements in the heap. These structures enable quick prioritization and efficient task management.

Disjoint Set (Union-Find)

Disjoint Set, often referred to as Union-Find, is a fundamental data structure used to manage a collection of disjoint (non-overlapping) sets. It excels at answering questions related to set membership and efficiently determining connected components within a larger structure, making it a versatile tool for a wide range of applications.

Understanding Disjoint Set:

Disjoint Set is designed to address problems related to grouping and partitioning elements into sets, while also allowing for efficient querying of set membership. It maintains a collection of disjoint sets, each represented by a unique root element. The key operations in Disjoint Set are:

- **MakeSet:** Create a new set with a single element. Initially, each element is its own set, and its representative is itself.
- **Union (UnionFind):** Merge two sets into one by connecting the roots of their representative elements.
- **Find (FindSet):** Determine the representative (root) element of a set to which a given element belongs. This operation is used to check set membership.

The Union-Find Data Structure:

The Union-Find data structure represents sets as disjoint trees. Each element within a set is a node in the tree, with the root node serving as the representative element. The structure maintains a parent-pointer hierarchy, enabling efficient Union and Find operations.

Path Compression:

To optimize the Find operation, a technique known as path compression can be applied. Path compression involves flattening the tree structure by making every node in the path from the queried element to the root point directly to the root. This significantly reduces the depth of the tree and speeds up future Find operations.

Applications of Disjoint Set:

Disjoint Set finds applications in various domains, including:

1. **Connectivity Analysis:** Disjoint Set efficiently determines whether two elements are in the same connected component or not. It is widely used in network analysis, image processing, and graph algorithms.
2. **Minimum Spanning Tree:** Kruskal's algorithm for finding the minimum spanning tree of a graph relies on Disjoint Set to identify and merge connected components.
3. **Image Segmentation:** In computer vision, Disjoint Set can be used to partition an image into distinct regions or objects.
4. **Union-Find in Competitive Programming:** It is a valuable tool for solving coding problems involving set unions and set membership queries.

Performance Analysis:

When path compression is employed, the amortized time complexity of both Union and Find operations in Disjoint Set is approximately $O(\alpha(n))$, where $\alpha(n)$ is the extremely slow-growing inverse Ackermann function. In practical terms, this means Disjoint Set offers nearly constant-time performance for these operations.

Trie Data Structure

The Trie (pronounced as "try") data structure is a powerful and versatile tool for efficiently storing and retrieving a large collection of words or strings. It excels at tasks involving searching, auto-completion, and spell checking.

Understanding the Trie:

A Trie, short for "reTRIEval tree," is a tree-like data structure used primarily for managing and searching through a set of strings. Unlike many other data structures, Trie nodes do not store individual elements; instead, they represent the characters of the stored strings. Each node typically has links to child nodes, each corresponding to a character in the alphabet.

Trie Construction:

The construction of a Trie involves adding words one character at a time. Each character is represented by a node, and as more words are added, the Trie grows dynamically. The root node represents an empty string, and subsequent nodes represent the characters of the words in the Trie.

Searching in a Trie:

Searching for a word in a Trie is efficient and straightforward. Starting from the root, you traverse the Trie by following the edges that correspond to each character in the target word. If you reach the end of the word and the node you're on is marked as a valid word (i.e., it represents the end of a stored word), you have successfully found the word.

Insertion and Deletion:

Inserting a word into a Trie is also straightforward. You start at the root and add nodes for each character in the word, following existing branches where possible. Deletion is similarly straightforward by removing nodes corresponding to characters. However, Trie deletion can be more complex when considering how it affects other words in the Trie.

Efficiency of Trie:

Tries are highly efficient for various string-related tasks, such as:

- **Auto-completion:** Tries are often used to provide auto-completion suggestions as you type, making them crucial in search engines and text editors.
- **Spell Checking:** Tries can be employed to check the spelling of words in a document efficiently.
- **Searching for Prefixes:** Tries excel at searching for words with a common prefix, such as finding all words that start with "pre."

Applications of Tries:

Trie data structures find applications in various domains, including:

- **Dictionaries:** Many dictionary implementations use Tries to store and look up words efficiently.
- **Contact List in Mobile Phones:** Tries are used to provide auto-completion and searching in contact lists.
- **Network Routing:** IP address routing tables often use Tries for efficient lookups.

Performance Analysis:

The time complexity for searching, insertion, and deletion in a Trie is O(m), where m is the length of the target word. This makes Tries highly efficient for operations involving strings of varying lengths.

ALGORITHM DESIGN TECHNIQUES

Greedy Algorithms

Greedy algorithms are a class of algorithms that make a series of locally optimal choices to arrive at a globally optimal solution. They are simple, intuitive, and often provide efficient solutions to a wide range of problems.

Understanding Greedy Algorithms:

At the core of greedy algorithms lies a simple philosophy: make the best choice available at each step, hoping that these locally optimal choices will lead to a globally optimal solution. Greedy algorithms do not backtrack or reconsider previous decisions, making decisions based solely on current information.

Key Characteristics of Greedy Algorithms:

1. **Greedy Choice Property:** Greedy algorithms make decisions based on the best available option at each step without considering the consequences of those choices in the long run. This property simplifies the decision-making process.
2. **Optimal Substructure:** Greedy algorithms rely on the assumption that making the best choice at each step will result in an overall optimal solution. This is often expressed as the problem having an "optimal substructure."

Examples of Greedy Algorithms:

1. **Dijkstra's Shortest Path Algorithm:** Dijkstra's algorithm finds the shortest path from a source node to all other nodes in a weighted graph. It uses a priority queue to select the node with the smallest distance at each step.
2. **Huffman Coding:** Huffman coding is used for data compression, where characters are assigned variable-length codes based on their frequency of

occurrence. Greedy choices are made to construct an optimal binary tree for encoding.

3. **Minimum Spanning Trees:** Algorithms like Kruskal's and Prim's are used to find minimum spanning trees in graphs, ensuring the most efficient way to connect all nodes while minimizing the total edge weight.
4. **Interval Scheduling:** In scheduling problems, greedy algorithms are applied to select a maximum number of non-overlapping intervals, such as in classroom scheduling or job scheduling.

Performance Analysis:

The efficiency of greedy algorithms often depends on the specific problem they are applied to. When greedy algorithms are applicable, they can provide solutions with excellent time complexity, typically linear or better. However, their greedy nature does not guarantee optimality for every problem, so careful consideration of the problem's characteristics is essential.

When to Use Greedy Algorithms:

Greedy algorithms are most effective when the greedy choice property and optimal substructure are present in the problem. However, they may not always yield the optimal solution. It's essential to evaluate whether a greedy approach is appropriate for a given problem.

Divide and Conquer

Divide and Conquer is a powerful algorithmic paradigm that divides a complex problem into smaller, more manageable subproblems, solves them recursively, and combines their solutions to produce the final result. This approach is widely used to solve a diverse range of problems efficiently.

Understanding Divide and Conquer:

At its core, Divide and Conquer is about breaking down a problem into smaller, simpler instances that are easier to solve. It follows a three-step process:

1. **Divide:** Break the problem into smaller, non-overlapping subproblems of the same type.
2. **Conquer:** Solve each subproblem individually, typically by applying the same algorithm recursively.
3. **Combine:** Merge the solutions of the subproblems to obtain the solution to the original problem.

Key Characteristics of Divide and Conquer:

1. **Recursive Approach:** Divide and Conquer relies on recursive function calls to solve subproblems. The base case defines when to stop the recursion.
2. **Optimal Substructure:** The problem must exhibit an optimal substructure, meaning that the solution to the original problem can be expressed in terms of solutions to its subproblems.

Examples of Divide and Conquer:

1. **Merge Sort:** Merge Sort is a classic example of a Divide and Conquer algorithm used for sorting arrays. It divides the array into two halves, sorts them recursively, and then merges the sorted halves to produce a sorted array.
2. **Binary Search:** Binary Search is a Divide and Conquer algorithm used to search for an element in a sorted array. It repeatedly divides the search space in half, eliminating the half where the target cannot exist.
3. **Fast Fourier Transform (FFT):** FFT is used to efficiently compute the discrete Fourier transform of a sequence. It divides the problem into smaller subproblems and combines their results using complex mathematical operations.
4. **Matrix Multiplication:** The Strassen algorithm is a Divide and Conquer method for multiplying matrices efficiently by breaking down matrix multiplication into smaller submatrix multiplications.

Performance Analysis:

Divide and Conquer algorithms often exhibit efficient time complexity, depending on the problem and how it is divided. In many cases, they achieve a time complexity of $O(n \log n)$, making them highly efficient for large datasets.

When to Use Divide and Conquer:

Divide and Conquer is suitable for problems with a natural recursive structure and optimal substructure. It excels in problems that can be divided into smaller, independent parts that can be solved separately and then combined to find the overall solution.

Dynamic Programming

Dynamic Programming (DP) is a powerful problem-solving technique that combines recursion and memoization to efficiently solve problems by breaking them down into smaller overlapping subproblems. It is especially useful for optimizing recursive algorithms and solving a wide range of computational problems.

Understanding Dynamic Programming:

Dynamic Programming is about solving problems by breaking them into smaller, overlapping subproblems and efficiently solving each subproblem only once. It emphasizes reusing solutions to subproblems to avoid redundant computation. DP problems are typically solved using a bottom-up or top-down approach.

Key Characteristics of Dynamic Programming:

1. **Optimal Substructure:** Like other algorithmic paradigms, DP relies on the assumption that optimal solutions to larger problems can be constructed from optimal solutions to smaller subproblems. This property is known as an optimal substructure.
2. **Memoization:** DP employs memoization, which involves storing solutions to subproblems in a data structure (usually an array or a table) to avoid recalculating them when needed again. This dramatically reduces computational overhead.

Examples of Dynamic Programming:

1. **Fibonacci Sequence:** The Fibonacci sequence is a classic DP problem. DP efficiently computes Fibonacci numbers by storing previously computed values in an array to avoid redundant calculations.
2. **Longest Common Subsequence (LCS):** In the LCS problem, DP is used to find the longest subsequence shared between two sequences, often used in DNA sequence alignment and text comparison.
3. **Knapsack Problem:** DP can solve the 0/1 Knapsack problem efficiently, where items have weights and values, and you need to find the maximum value of items to fit in a knapsack of limited capacity.
4. **Shortest Path Problems:** DP algorithms like Floyd-Warshall and Bellman-Ford find shortest paths in weighted graphs, essential in network routing and navigation.

Performance Analysis:

The efficiency of DP algorithms is a result of avoiding redundant computations through memoization. DP algorithms typically achieve time complexities ranging from linear to polynomial, depending on the problem.

When to Use Dynamic Programming:

Dynamic Programming is most effective when a problem exhibits an overlapping substructure, meaning that it can be divided into smaller subproblems, and solutions to these subproblems are reused multiple times. DP is also applicable when you need to optimize a recursive algorithm.

Backtracking

Backtracking is a problem-solving technique that systematically explores all possible solutions to a problem by incrementally building a solution and undoing it if it's determined to be invalid. This approach is particularly useful for solving problems with multiple decision points and constraints.

Understanding Backtracking:

Backtracking is often likened to a maze-solving strategy where you explore different paths, backtrack when you reach a dead-end, and continue exploring until you find a solution or exhaust all possibilities. It involves making a series of choices at each decision point and backtracking when those choices lead to invalid solutions.

Key Characteristics of Backtracking:

1. **Recursive Approach:** Backtracking is typically implemented recursively. The algorithm explores each possibility by making choices, recursing deeper into the problem, and backtracking to try other options if necessary.
2. **Decision Points:** Problems suitable for backtracking have multiple decision points where choices must be made. These decisions lead to different branches in the exploration tree.

Examples of Backtracking:

1. **N-Queens Problem:** Backtracking is often used to solve the N-Queens problem, where you must place N queens on an N×N chessboard so that no two queens threaten each other.
2. **Sudoku Solving:** Sudoku puzzles can be solved using backtracking by trying different numbers in each cell and backtracking when an invalid solution is encountered.
3. **Word Search:** Backtracking is employed to search for words in a grid of letters, moving through adjacent cells to form valid words.
4. **Combinatorial Problems:** Problems like generating all permutations, combinations, or subsets of a set are commonly solved using backtracking.

Performance Analysis:

The efficiency of backtracking algorithms depends on the problem and the pruning techniques applied. In the worst case, where all possibilities are explored, the time complexity can be exponential. However, intelligent pruning strategies can significantly reduce the search space.

When to Use Backtracking:

Backtracking is most effective when a problem involves making a series of choices with constraints and multiple possible paths. It is applicable when you need to search through a solution space exhaustively.

Introduction to Complexity Classes (P vs NP)

In computer science and algorithmic theory, the concept of complexity classes plays a central role in understanding the efficiency and solvability of computational problems. One of the most famous and intriguing questions in this field is the P vs NP problem, which explores the fundamental distinction between problems that can be quickly solved and those that may not have efficient solutions.

What Are Complexity Classes?

Complexity classes are sets of computational problems grouped by their inherent computational difficulty. These classes provide a framework for categorizing problems based on how their time and space requirements scale with input size. Two fundamental complexity classes are P and NP:

- **P (Polynomial Time):** Problems in class P are those for which a solution can be found in polynomial time, meaning that their time complexity is bounded by a polynomial function of the input size.
- **NP (Nondeterministic Polynomial Time):** Problems in class NP are those for which a proposed solution can be verified in polynomial time. In other words, if someone gives you a potential solution, you can quickly check its correctness.

The P vs NP Problem:

The P vs NP problem is a major unsolved question in computer science and mathematics. It asks whether every problem in NP is also in P, meaning that problems with efficiently verifiable solutions also have efficient algorithms for finding those solutions.

- **P:** If P equals NP, it implies that problems with efficient solutions (P) also have efficient verification methods (NP). In practical terms, this would mean that problems for which we can easily check solutions could also be solved efficiently.
- **P ≠ NP:** If P is not equal to NP, it suggests that there are problems in NP for which efficient solutions are unlikely to exist. In this scenario, finding efficient algorithms for NP-complete problems (a subset of NP) would be an extraordinary achievement.

Significance of P vs NP:

The P vs NP problem is considered one of the seven "Millennium Prize Problems," and it has far-reaching implications in computer science and cryptography. Its resolution would answer whether certain problems, like the traveling salesman problem and the Boolean satisfiability problem, can be solved efficiently. Furthermore, the P vs NP problem has profound implications for cryptography, as many encryption methods rely on the assumption that certain problems are hard to solve (NP-complete).

The Impact on Computing:

If P equals NP, it would revolutionize computing by providing efficient solutions to problems that are currently considered computationally intractable. On the other hand, if P is not equal to NP, it would affirm the existence of problems that are inherently difficult to solve efficiently.

ADVANCED TOPICS

Graph Algorithms

Graphs are a fundamental data structure used to model relationships and connections between entities. Whether you're planning the shortest route for a GPS application or optimizing a network's infrastructure, graph algorithms are the tools of choice.

The Shortest Path Problem:

The shortest path problem involves finding the most efficient route between two nodes in a weighted graph. This problem has widespread applications, from GPS navigation to network routing and logistics optimization.

- **Dijkstra's Algorithm:** Named after its inventor Edsger W. Dijkstra, this algorithm finds the shortest path from a starting node to all other nodes in a non-negative weighted graph. Dijkstra's algorithm employs a priority queue to iteratively select the node with the shortest known distance.
- **Bellman-Ford Algorithm:** Unlike Dijkstra's algorithm, Bellman-Ford can handle graphs with negative weight edges but is less efficient. It iterates through all edges multiple times, relaxing them to update the shortest distances.

The Minimum Spanning Tree:

A minimum spanning tree (MST) is a subset of edges in a graph that connects all nodes while minimizing the total edge weight. MSTs find applications in network design, clustering, and circuit optimization.

- **Kruskal's Algorithm:** Kruskal's algorithm is a greedy approach to finding an MST. It starts with an empty set of edges and iteratively adds the edge with the lowest weight that doesn't create a cycle.

- **Prim's Algorithm:** Prim's algorithm also constructs an MST incrementally, starting from an arbitrary node and adding edges that connect the MST to the remaining nodes with the lowest weight.

Performance Analysis:

The efficiency of graph algorithms depends on various factors, including the size of the graph, the distribution of edge weights, and the algorithm used. Dijkstra's algorithm and Prim's algorithm typically achieve a time complexity of $O(V^2)$ or $O(V \log V)$, depending on the implementation. Kruskal's algorithm and Bellman-Ford have slightly higher complexities due to their edge-centric nature.

Real-World Applications:

These graph algorithms are the backbone of modern transportation systems, telecommunications networks, and data analysis platforms. They enable efficient routing in GPS devices, connectivity analysis in social networks, and network design in communication infrastructure.

Advanced Searching Techniques: KMP and Rabin-Karp

Searching for patterns within text is a common problem in computer science and information retrieval. While basic search algorithms like linear search serve well for small datasets, they can become highly inefficient when searching large texts.

The Knuth-Morris-Pratt (KMP) Algorithm:

The KMP algorithm is a string matching algorithm that efficiently finds all occurrences of a given pattern within a text. What sets KMP apart is its ability to avoid unnecessary character comparisons during the search, making it particularly efficient for large texts.

- **Pattern Preprocessing:** The KMP algorithm preprocesses the pattern to construct a partial match table (also known as the failure function) that helps it skip unnecessary character comparisons.
- **Efficient Search:** During the search phase, KMP uses the information from the partial match table to avoid comparing characters that are guaranteed not to match, significantly reducing the number of comparisons.

The Rabin-Karp Algorithm:

The Rabin-Karp algorithm is a string searching algorithm that employs hashing to search for patterns within text. It uses a rolling hash function to compute the hash values of the pattern and sliding window in the text efficiently.

- **Hashing for Pattern and Text:** Rabin-Karp computes hash values for the pattern and a moving window of text characters. It then compares these hash values, eliminating unnecessary character-by-character comparisons.
- **Rolling Hash:** As the window slides, Rabin-Karp efficiently updates the hash value by removing the trailing character's contribution and adding the new character's contribution.

Performance Analysis:

The efficiency of these searching techniques depends on various factors, including the length of the text, the length of the pattern, and the nature of the data. In general, KMP has a time complexity of $O(N+M)$, where N is the length of the text, and M is the length of the pattern. Rabin-Karp also has an average-case time complexity of $O(N+M)$, but its performance can degrade if not implemented carefully.

Real-World Applications:

KMP and Rabin-Karp are used extensively in text processing applications like text editors, search engines, and data deduplication systems. They help efficiently identify and locate patterns within vast volumes of text data.

Computational Geometry

Computational geometry is a fascinating subfield of computer science that combines mathematical principles with algorithmic techniques to solve a wide range of geometric problems. From finding the convex hull of a set of points to determining the intersection of geometric shapes, computational geometry plays a vital role in various applications, including computer graphics, robotics, geographic information systems (GIS), and more.

The World of Geometric Problems:

Geometry is all about understanding the properties and relationships of shapes and figures in space. Computational geometry takes this a step further by introducing algorithms to address complex geometric problems.

Foundations of Computational Geometry:

1. **Convex Hull:** One of the fundamental problems in computational geometry is finding the convex hull of a set of points. The convex hull is the smallest convex polygon that encloses all given points. Algorithms like Graham's scan and QuickHull efficiently compute the convex hull.
2. **Closest Pair of Points:** Given a set of points, the closest pair of points problem involves finding the two points that are closest to each other. Techniques like the divide and conquer approach can be used to solve this problem efficiently.
3. **Geometric Intersection:** Computational geometry deals with determining the intersection points and areas of geometric shapes, such as line segments, polygons, and circles. Algorithms for line segment intersection and polygon intersection are crucial in various applications, including GIS and computer graphics.

Applications of Computational Geometry:

1. **Computer Graphics:** In computer graphics, computational geometry is used to render and manipulate 2D and 3D objects efficiently. It enables tasks like hidden surface removal, collision detection, and realistic rendering.
2. **Robotics:** Robots often rely on computational geometry to navigate their environment, avoid obstacles, and plan efficient paths.
3. **GIS and Cartography:** Geographic information systems (GIS) use computational geometry to analyze and visualize spatial data, such as maps, satellite images, and terrain models.
4. **Manufacturing and CNC Machining:** Computational geometry helps design and control the movement of machine tools in computer numerical control (CNC) machining, ensuring precise and efficient manufacturing processes.

Performance Analysis:

The efficiency of computational geometry algorithms depends on factors like the number of geometric elements, the complexity of shapes, and the chosen algorithm. Some problems can be solved in linear or logarithmic time, while others have polynomial or even exponential complexity.

NP-Hard and NP-Complete Problems

In algorithmic complexity, some problems stand out as particularly challenging. Among them are NP-hard and NP-complete problems. These classes of problems play a crucial role in computer science and mathematics, pushing the boundaries of what can be efficiently computed.

Complexity Classes and Problem Classification:

To appreciate NP-hard and NP-complete problems, it's essential to understand the classification of computational problems based on their computational complexity. Problems are categorized into different complexity classes, including P, NP, NP-hard, and NP-complete:

- **P (Polynomial Time):** Problems in this class can be solved efficiently, with their time complexity bounded by a polynomial function of the input size.
- **NP (Nondeterministic Polynomial Time):** Problems in this class can be verified efficiently once a solution is proposed. They may or may not be solvable efficiently.

What Are NP-Hard Problems?

A problem is classified as NP-hard (nondeterministic polynomial-time hard) if it is at least as hard as the hardest problems in NP. In other words, if you can solve an NP-hard problem efficiently, you can potentially solve all problems in NP efficiently.

What Are NP-Complete Problems?

NP-complete (nondeterministic polynomial-time complete) problems are a subset of NP-hard problems with a special property: they are among the hardest problems in NP. An NP-complete problem is both in NP and as hard as the hardest problems in NP. The most famous NP-complete problem is the Boolean satisfiability problem (SAT).

Implications of NP-Complete Problems:

The discovery of NP-complete problems by Stephen Cook and Leonid Levin in the 1970s had a profound impact on computer science and mathematics. The most significant implication is the concept of "NP-completeness reduction." If you can prove that an NP-complete problem can be reduced to another problem, it implies that the second problem is also NP-complete.

Cook's Theorem and P vs. NP:

Stephen Cook's groundbreaking work, which established the concept of NP-completeness, is the foundation for the P vs. NP question. This question asks whether P (problems solvable in polynomial time) is the same as NP (problems verifiable in polynomial time). If P equals NP, it implies that all NP problems are also solvable in polynomial time, revolutionizing computing. However, if P is not equal to NP, it suggests that there are problems in NP that are inherently hard to solve efficiently.

Real-World Applications:

NP-hard and NP-complete problems have far-reaching implications in various domains, including optimization, cryptography, and artificial intelligence. For instance, the traveling salesman problem, an NP-complete problem, arises in route planning and logistics optimization.

JAVA LIBRARIES AND FRAMEWORKS

Java Collections Framework

In Java programming, efficient data management is an important aspect of software development. Java's Collections Framework provides a robust and comprehensive set of tools for managing and manipulating collections of objects.

Understanding the Collections Framework:

The Java Collections Framework is a unified architecture for representing and manipulating collections of objects. It offers a consistent and efficient way to work with data structures, making it easier to organize and process data in Java programs.

Key Components of the Collections Framework:

1. **Interfaces:** At the heart of the Collections Framework are several interfaces that define various types of collections. These interfaces include List, Set, Map, Queue, and more. Each interface provides a different way of organizing and accessing data.
2. **Classes:** The framework includes concrete implementations of these interfaces, such as ArrayList, HashSet, HashMap, and LinkedList. These classes offer ready-to-use data structures that adhere to the respective interfaces.

Benefits of the Collections Framework:

1. **Consistency:** The framework enforces a consistent API across different collection types, making it easier to switch between implementations as needed.
2. **Efficiency:** Collections are optimized for performance, ensuring that common operations like adding, retrieving, and removing elements are as efficient as possible.

3. **Safety:** The framework provides type safety, preventing the inadvertent mixing of different data types in a collection.

Commonly Used Collection Types:

1. **List:** Lists allow you to store ordered collections of elements. Common implementations include ArrayList, LinkedList, and Vector.
2. **Set:** Sets store unique elements, ensuring that duplicates are not allowed. Popular implementations are HashSet and TreeSet.
3. **Map:** Maps store key-value pairs and allow efficient retrieval of values based on keys. The HashMap and TreeMap are widely used implementations.

Iterating Through Collections:

The Collections Framework provides a standard way to iterate through elements using iterators or enhanced for-each loops, making it convenient to access and process data within collections.

Real-World Applications:

The Java Collections Framework is a crucial component in various Java applications and libraries. It simplifies tasks like data storage, manipulation, and retrieval, making it invaluable in scenarios ranging from database interactions to user interface development.

Java Streams API

Java Streams offer a powerful and expressive way to work with collections of data, allowing developers to perform complex data transformations with simplicity and efficiency.

The Evolution of Data Processing:

Traditionally, processing data in Java involved loops and iterative constructs, which, while functional, often led to verbose and error-prone code. The Streams API was introduced in Java 8 to address these challenges and provide a more elegant and efficient way to process data.

Key Concepts of the Streams API:

1. **Stream:** A stream is a sequence of data elements that can be processed in a functional-style manner. Streams can be created from collections, arrays, or by generating elements individually.
2. **Intermediate and Terminal Operations:** Streams support two types of operations: intermediate and terminal. Intermediate operations transform a stream into another stream (e.g., map, filter), while terminal operations produce a result or a side-effect (e.g., collect, forEach).
3. **Functional Programming:** Streams encourage a functional programming paradigm, where data is treated as immutable and processed through a series of transformations, rather than being modified in-place.

Benefits of Using Streams:

1. **Readability:** Streams code is often more concise and readable compared to traditional loop-based approaches, making it easier to understand and maintain.
2. **Parallelism:** Streams can be easily parallelized, allowing for efficient multicore processing and potentially significant performance improvements.
3. **Immutable Data:** Streams promote immutability, reducing the risk of data corruption and making code more predictable.

Common Stream Operations:

1. **Mapping:** The map operation transforms each element in a stream by applying a given function to it.
2. **Filtering:** The filter operation selects elements from a stream that satisfy a specified condition.
3. **Reduction:** The reduce operation combines elements in a stream to produce a single result, such as summing numbers or finding the maximum value.
4. **Collecting:** The collect operation accumulates elements from a stream into a collection or performs other types of reduction.

Real-World Applications:

Java Streams are widely used in various domains, including data processing, data analysis, and web development. They simplify tasks like filtering and transforming data, making them invaluable in scenarios like data analytics, web service requests, and database queries.

Third-party Libraries for Data Structures and Algorithms: Expanding Your Toolkit

The Quest for Efficiency and Specialization:

While the Java standard library offers a broad range of data structures and algorithms, there are scenarios where specialized libraries provide significant advantages. Third-party libraries often focus on performance optimization, unique data structures, or specific problem domains, making them invaluable in certain contexts.

Popular Third-party Libraries:

1. **Apache Commons Collections:** Apache Commons Collections is a well-known library that complements the Java Collections Framework with additional data structures and utilities. It offers enhanced collections like Bag, BidiMap, and MultiMap, along with various utilities for manipulation.
2. **Guava (Google Core Libraries for Java):** Developed by Google, Guava provides a wide array of utilities and data structures not found in the standard library. It includes collections like BiMap and Table, as well as functional programming constructs and other helpful tools.
3. **JGraphT:** JGraphT is a powerful library for graph data structures and algorithms. It provides an extensive set of graph types, algorithms for traversal and connectivity analysis, and support for various graph representations.
4. **JAMA (Java Matrix Package):** JAMA is a library for linear algebra operations, including matrix decompositions, solving linear systems of equations, and performing eigenvalue computations.
5. **Jedis (Java Redis Client):** If you work with Redis, a popular in-memory data store, Jedis provides a Java client library to interact with Redis servers efficiently.

Benefits of Third-party Libraries:

1. **Specialized Data Structures:** Third-party libraries offer specialized data structures tailored to specific use cases, such as spatial indexing, quad trees, or specialized graph types.
2. **Performance Optimization:** These libraries often focus on performance optimization, ensuring that data structures and algorithms are highly efficient for particular tasks.

3. **Rich Functionality:** Many third-party libraries extend the functionality of the Java standard library, providing additional utilities and tools for common programming challenges.

Integration and Compatibility:

Integrating third-party libraries into your Java projects is generally straightforward. Most libraries are available via popular package managers like Maven or Gradle, simplifying dependency management.

Real-World Applications:

Third-party libraries for data structures and algorithms find applications in various domains, including game development, scientific computing, geographic information systems (GIS), and more. Their specialization and performance enhancements make them invaluable in scenarios where standard libraries may not suffice.

BEST PRACTICES AND TIPS

Code Optimization: Enhancing Efficiency and Performance

Efficiency and performance are two essential aspects of software development. In the realm of Java programming, optimizing your code is a crucial skill that can lead to faster execution, reduced resource consumption, and a more responsive user experience.

Optimizing code isn't just about making it run faster; it's also about using system resources more judiciously and reducing the overall footprint of your application. Whether you're building a desktop application, a web service, or a mobile app, code optimization is a fundamental step in delivering a high-quality product.

Key Code Optimization Techniques:

1. **Algorithm Selection:** Choose the right algorithms and data structures for your specific problem. The choice of algorithm can have a profound impact on the efficiency of your code.
2. **Avoid Premature Optimization:** Don't optimize prematurely. Focus on writing clear, maintainable code first, and then identify performance bottlenecks using profiling tools.
3. **Profiling:** Use profiling tools to identify performance bottlenecks in your code. Profilers can help pinpoint which parts of your code are consuming the most time and resources.
4. **Memory Management:** Be mindful of memory usage. Avoid unnecessary object creation, use object pooling where applicable, and release resources explicitly when they are no longer needed.
5. **Concurrency:** Leverage multithreading and concurrency when appropriate to take advantage of modern hardware. Be cautious of synchronization overhead and race conditions.

6. **I/O Optimization:** Optimize input and output operations, such as file I/O and network communication, to minimize latency and maximize throughput.
7. **Caching:** Implement caching mechanisms to store frequently accessed data in memory, reducing the need for expensive computations or database queries.

Code Optimization Best Practices:

1. **Measure Before You Optimize:** Always measure and profile your code before attempting optimization. Identify the actual bottlenecks rather than guessing where optimizations are needed.
2. **Focus on Hotspots:** Concentrate your optimization efforts on the portions of your code that consume the most resources and have the greatest impact on performance.
3. **Use Benchmarking:** Create meaningful benchmarks to compare the performance of different implementations or optimizations.
4. **Maintain Code Readability:** Code optimization should not sacrifice code readability and maintainability. Ensure that your optimized code remains clear and well-documented.
5. **Iterative Approach:** Optimize your code iteratively. Make incremental changes, measure the impact, and fine-tune as necessary.

Code optimization is critical in scenarios where performance is a top priority, such as video game development, financial applications, scientific simulations, and web servers. Even in less performance-critical applications, efficient code can lead to better user experiences and reduced operational costs.

Debugging and Testing: Ensuring Code Reliability and Quality

Ensuring that your code works as intended, performs efficiently, and remains free of errors is important. Debugging and testing are the essential processes that help you achieve these goals in Java programming.

The Role of Debugging and Testing:

Debugging and testing are two inseparable pillars of software development. They serve distinct but complementary purposes:

- **Debugging:** Debugging is the process of identifying and fixing errors, also known as bugs, in your code. It involves tracking down issues that prevent your program from functioning correctly and correcting them.
- **Testing:** Testing is the systematic process of evaluating your code to ensure it meets the specified requirements and performs reliably. Testing aims to verify that the software behaves as expected under different scenarios.

Key Debugging Techniques:

1. **Use a Debugger:** Java provides powerful debugging tools like the Java Debugger (jdb) and integrated development environments (IDEs) with debugging support. These tools allow you to step through your code, inspect variables, and set breakpoints to identify and fix issues.
2. **Logging:** Incorporate logging statements into your code using frameworks like Log4j or the built-in java.util.logging. Logging helps you record program behavior and pinpoint errors by examining log outputs.
3. **Unit Testing:** Write unit tests using testing frameworks like JUnit or TestNG to verify the correctness of individual components or methods in isolation.
4. **Integration Testing:** Conduct integration tests to ensure that different components of your application work together seamlessly. This involves testing the interactions between modules or services.
5. **Regression Testing:** Implement regression tests to verify that new code changes do not introduce new bugs or break existing functionality.

Testing Levels and Strategies:

1. **Unit Testing:** Focuses on testing individual units or functions in isolation. It is crucial for verifying the correctness of small code components.
2. **Integration Testing:** Tests the interactions and interfaces between different modules or services within an application.
3. **Functional Testing:** Evaluates whether the software performs its intended functions correctly. It typically involves testing the entire application or system.
4. **Performance Testing:** Assesses the system's response time, scalability, and resource consumption under various loads and conditions.

Automated Testing:

Automated testing using frameworks like JUnit, TestNG, and Selenium enables you to run tests consistently and efficiently. Automated tests can be incorporated into your continuous integration (CI) and continuous delivery (CD) pipelines to ensure that code changes are thoroughly tested before deployment.

Test-Driven Development (TDD):

TDD is a development methodology where tests are written before the code itself. By following TDD principles, developers ensure that code is thoroughly tested and meets the specified requirements from the outset.

Effective debugging and testing are critical for all types of Java applications, from desktop software and web applications to mobile apps and microservices. Reliable and well-tested code is essential to provide a smooth and error-free user experience.

Handling Edge Cases

While your code may work flawlessly in typical situations, it must also gracefully handle edge cases—those unexpected and often unusual scenarios that can challenge the stability and reliability of your software.

What Are Edge Cases?

Edge cases refer to scenarios that lie at the extreme or boundary conditions of your software's expected behavior. These cases often involve inputs, circumstances, or conditions that your code may not have been explicitly designed to handle.

Why Handle Edge Cases?

Handling edge cases is crucial for several reasons:

1. **Robustness:** Robust software can withstand unexpected inputs or conditions without crashing or producing incorrect results. Handling edge cases contributes to your application's robustness.
2. **User Experience:** Unexpected behavior, errors, or crashes can result in a poor user experience. Handling edge cases helps ensure that users don't encounter unexpected issues.
3. **Security:** Failing to address edge cases can lead to vulnerabilities that attackers could exploit. Security-conscious coding includes handling edge cases to protect your application.

Common Edge Case Scenarios:

1. **Input Validation:** Check user inputs for correctness and validity. Handling invalid inputs gracefully prevents issues caused by incorrect data.
2. **Boundary Values:** Consider boundary values when working with loops, arrays, and data ranges. Test your code with the lowest and highest values permitted.
3. **Resource Exhaustion:** Be prepared for scenarios where system resources (memory, CPU, disk space) may become limited or exhausted. Implement resource management strategies.
4. **Concurrency Issues:** When working with multithreaded applications, handle race conditions, deadlocks, and thread synchronization issues.
5. **Network and I/O Failures:** Address network timeouts, slow connections, and I/O errors to prevent your application from hanging or crashing.

Strategies for Handling Edge Cases:

1. **Validation and Sanitization:** Validate and sanitize user inputs to ensure they meet expected criteria. Reject or handle invalid inputs gracefully.
2. **Exception Handling:** Use exception handling to capture and handle unexpected errors or exceptional conditions. Provide meaningful error messages and log details for debugging.
3. **Fallback Mechanisms:** Implement fallback mechanisms to handle situations where primary resources or services are unavailable. Use defaults or alternative methods when necessary.
4. **Graceful Degradation:** In web applications, consider implementing graceful degradation, where the application provides a reduced but functional experience when certain features or resources are unavailable.
5. **Logging and Monitoring:** Implement extensive logging and monitoring to track application behavior and performance. This helps detect and address edge cases in production.

Edge case handling is essential in all types of software, from web applications and mobile apps to server-side services and embedded systems. It ensures that your software remains reliable and user-friendly even when faced with unusual circumstances.

Choosing the Right Data Structure and Algorithm

Effective programming is not just about writing code that works; it's about writing code that works efficiently. Choosing the right data structures and algorithms is a critical decision that can significantly impact the performance and scalability of your Java applications.

The Importance of Choosing Wisely:

The choice of data structure and algorithm is akin to selecting the right tool for a job. Just as a carpenter wouldn't use a screwdriver to drive a nail, a developer should choose data structures and algorithms that align with the problem's requirements and constraints.

Factors to Consider:

When choosing data structures and algorithms, consider the following factors:

1. **Problem Complexity:** Understand the complexity of the problem you're solving. Some problems are simple and can be solved with basic data structures, while others require more advanced algorithms.
2. **Input Size:** Consider the size of the input data. Algorithms that perform well with small datasets may not scale effectively to large datasets.
3. **Time Constraints:** Determine if your application has strict time constraints. Real-time applications often require algorithms with low time complexity.
4. **Space Constraints:** Assess whether your application has limited memory resources. In memory-constrained environments, minimizing space complexity is crucial.
5. **Expected Operations:** Identify the types of operations your application will perform most frequently. Choose data structures optimized for these operations.

Common Data Structures and Algorithms:

1. **Arrays:** Arrays are suitable for simple data storage and offer constant-time access to elements by index.
2. **Lists:** Linked lists and arrays lists are used for dynamic data storage. Linked lists excel at insertions and deletions, while array lists offer fast random access.
3. **Maps and Sets:** Maps (e.g., HashMap) store key-value pairs, while sets (e.g., HashSet) store unique elements. They are useful for quick lookups.
4. **Sorting Algorithms:** Choose from sorting algorithms like Quick Sort, Merge Sort, and others based on the specific sorting needs of your data.
5. **Search Algorithms:** Binary Search, Linear Search, and various search tree structures are available for efficient searching.

Trade-offs and Complexity:

Data structure and algorithm selection often involves trade-offs between time complexity and space complexity. For example, a more memory-efficient data structure may have higher time complexity for certain operations.

Choosing the right data structure and algorithm is essential in various domains, from web development and database management to artificial intelligence and game development. It impacts application performance, response times, and user experience.

INTERVIEW PREPARATION

Tips For Technical Interviews

Technical interviews can be nerve-wracking, especially when you're faced with challenging data structures and algorithms questions. However, with the right strategies and preparation, you can approach these interviews with confidence.

1. **Understand the Basics:** Before diving into complex problems, ensure you have a strong understanding of fundamental data structures (e.g., arrays, linked lists) and common algorithms (e.g., sorting, searching).

2. **Practice Regularly:** Consistent practice is key to success. Work through a variety of problems, ranging from easy to challenging, to strengthen your problem-solving skills.

3. **Master Time Complexity:** Understand the time complexity of common algorithms and be able to analyze the efficiency of your own code. Big O notation is your friend.

4. **Use Online Resources:** Leverage online coding platforms, websites, and resources that provide a plethora of coding challenges and interview questions.

5. **Mock Interviews:** Conduct mock interviews with peers, mentors, or online platforms to simulate the interview experience and receive constructive feedback.

6. **Whiteboard or Paper Coding:** Practice coding on a whiteboard or on paper. Technical interviews often involve writing code without the aid of an integrated development environment (IDE).

7. **Know Your Data Structures:** Be well-versed in data structures and their operations. Understand when to use each data structure based on the problem requirements.

8. **Plan Before You Code:** Always plan your approach before writing code. Outline the algorithm, consider edge cases, and validate your plan mentally.

9. **Start with Edge Cases:** When testing your code, begin with edge cases and boundary conditions to ensure your solution is robust.

10. **Ask Clarifying Questions:** In an interview, don't hesitate to ask clarifying questions if you're unsure about the problem statement or constraints. It demonstrates your problem-solving approach.

11. **Stay Calm and Communicate:** Maintain composure during interviews. Communicate your thought process clearly, even if you encounter difficulties. Interviewers appreciate transparency.

12. **Time Management:** Be mindful of time. If you're stuck on a particular problem, it's often better to move on and return to it later if time allows.

13. **Learn from Rejections:** If you don't succeed in an interview, view it as a learning opportunity. Ask for feedback, identify areas for improvement, and keep refining your skills.

14. **Behavioral Questions:** Prepare for behavioral questions as well. Interviewers may ask about your experiences, teamwork, and problem-solving approach.

15. **Stay Updated:** Keep abreast of new developments in the field of data structures and algorithms. Interviewers may inquire about recent advancements.

16. **Believe in Yourself:** Finally, believe in your abilities. Confidence in your problem-solving skills can make a significant difference in your interview performance.

The tips and strategies you learn during interview preparation aren't just for interviews. They improve your overall problem-solving skills and enhance your ability to write efficient and reliable code in professional software development projects.

Common Interview Questions and Solutions

1. **Reverse a Linked List:**
    - **Question**: Given a singly linked list, reverse it.
    - **Solution** :

```
class ListNode {
  int val;
  ListNode next;

  ListNode(int val) {
```

```java
    this.val = val;
  }
}

public ListNode reverseLinkedList(ListNode head) {
   ListNode prev = null;
   ListNode current = head;

   while (current != null) {
      ListNode next = current.next;
      current.next = prev;
      prev = current;
      current = next;
   }

   return prev;
}
```

2. **Find the Middle of a Linked List:**
    - **Question**: Find the middle node of a singly linked list.
    - **Solution** :

```java
public ListNode findMiddle(ListNode head) {
   ListNode slow = head;
   ListNode fast = head;

   while (fast != null && fast.next != null) {
      slow = slow.next;
      fast = fast.next.next;
   }

   return slow;
}
```

3. **Implement a Stack Using Linked List:**
    - **Question**: Implement a stack data structure using a singly linked list.
    - **Solution** :

```java
class StackNode {
   int data;
   StackNode next;

   StackNode(int data) {
      this.data = data;
   }
```

```java
}

class Stack {
   StackNode top;

   public void push(int data) {
      StackNode newNode = new StackNode(data);
      newNode.next = top;
      top = newNode;
   }

   public int pop() {
      if (isEmpty()) {
         throw new EmptyStackException();
      }
      int data = top.data;
      top = top.next;
      return data;
   }

   public boolean isEmpty() {
      return top == null;
   }
}
```

4. **Check for Palindrome:**
    - **Question**: Determine whether a given string is a palindrome.
    - **Solution** :

```java
public boolean isPalindrome(String s) {
   s = s.replaceAll("[^a-zA-Z0-9]", "").toLowerCase();
   int left = 0;
   int right = s.length() - 1;

   while (left < right) {
      if (s.charAt(left) != s.charAt(right)) {
         return false;
      }
      left++;
      right--;
   }

   return true;
}
```

5. **Binary Search:**
    - **Question**: Implement a binary search algorithm to find an element in a sorted array.
    - **Solution** :

```java
public int binarySearch(int[] arr, int target) {
   int left = 0;
   int right = arr.length - 1;

   while (left <= right) {
      int mid = left + (right - left) / 2;

      if (arr[mid] == target) {
         return mid;
      } else if (arr[mid] < target) {
         left = mid + 1;
      } else {
         right = mid - 1;
      }
   }

   return -1; // Element not found
}
```

6. **Merge Two Sorted Arrays**:
    - **Question**: Given two sorted arrays arr1 and arr2, merge them into a single sorted array.
    - **Solution** :

```java
public int[] mergeSortedArrays(int[] arr1, int[] arr2) {
   int[] result = new int[arr1.length + arr2.length];
   int i = 0, j = 0, k = 0;

   while (i < arr1.length && j < arr2.length) {
      if (arr1[i] <= arr2[j]) {
         result[k++] = arr1[i++];
      } else {
         result[k++] = arr2[j++];
      }
   }

   while (i < arr1.length) {
      result[k++] = arr1[i++];
   }
```

```
    while (j < arr2.length) {
        result[k++] = arr2[j++];
    }

    return result;
}
```

7. **Find the Intersection of Two Arrays**:
    - **Question**: Given two arrays, find their intersection (common elements).
    - **Solution** :

```
public int[] intersection(int[] nums1, int[] nums2) {
    Set<Integer> set = new HashSet<>();
    Set<Integer> intersection = new HashSet<>();

    for (int num : nums1) {
        set.add(num);
    }

    for (int num : nums2) {
        if (set.contains(num)) {
            intersection.add(num);
        }
    }

    int[] result = new int[intersection.size()];
    int i = 0;
    for (int num : intersection) {
        result[i++] = num;
    }

    return result;
}
```

8. **Implement a Queue Using Stacks**:
    - **Question**: Implement a queue data structure using two stacks.
    - **Solution** :

```
class MyQueue {
    Stack<Integer> inputStack;
    Stack<Integer> outputStack;
```

```java
    public MyQueue() {
        inputStack = new Stack<>();
        outputStack = new Stack<>();
    }

    public void push(int x) {
        inputStack.push(x);
    }

    public int pop() {
        if (outputStack.isEmpty()) {
            while (!inputStack.isEmpty()) {
                outputStack.push(inputStack.pop());
            }
        }
        return outputStack.pop();
    }

    public int peek() {
        if (outputStack.isEmpty()) {
            while (!inputStack.isEmpty()) {
                outputStack.push(inputStack.pop());
            }
        }
        return outputStack.peek();
    }

    public boolean empty() {
        return inputStack.isEmpty() && outputStack.isEmpty();
    }
}
```

9. **Find the Longest Substring Without Repeating Characters**.
    - **Question**: Given a string, find the length of the longest substring without repeating characters.
    - **Solution** :

```java
public int lengthOfLongestSubstring(String s) {
    int maxLen = 0;
    int left = 0;
    Map<Character, Integer> charIndexMap = new HashMap<>();

    for (int right = 0; right < s.length(); right++) {
        char c = s.charAt(right);
```

```
      if (charIndexMap.containsKey(c)) {
         left = Math.max(left, charIndexMap.get(c) + 1);
      }
      charIndexMap.put(c, right);
      maxLen = Math.max(maxLen, right - left + 1);
   }

   return maxLen;
}
```

10. **Topological Sort**:
    - **Question**: Implement the topological sorting algorithm for a directed graph.
    - **Solution** : You can implement topological sort using Depth-First Search (DFS) or Kahn's algorithm. Below is an example using Kahn's algorithm.

```
public List<Integer> topologicalSort(Graph graph) {
   List<Integer> result = new ArrayList<>();
   Queue<Integer> queue = new LinkedList<>();
   int[] inDegree = new int[graph.getNumVertices()];

   // Calculate in-degrees for each vertex
   for (int vertex = 0; vertex < graph.getNumVertices(); vertex++) {
      for (int neighbor : graph.getAdjacentVertices(vertex)) {
         inDegree[neighbor]++;
      }
   }

   // Enqueue vertices with in-degree 0
   for (int vertex = 0; vertex < graph.getNumVertices(); vertex++) {
      if (inDegree[vertex] == 0) {
         queue.add(vertex);
      }
   }

   // Perform topological sorting
   while (!queue.isEmpty()) {
      int vertex = queue.poll();
      result.add(vertex);

      for (int neighbor : graph.getAdjacentVertices(vertex)) {
         if (--inDegree[neighbor] == 0) {
            queue.add(neighbor);
```

```java
        }
      }
    }

    // Check for a cycle
    if (result.size() != graph.getNumVertices()) {
        throw new IllegalArgumentException("Graph contains a cycle!");
    }

    return result;
}
```

These common interview questions and solutions cover a wide range of data structures and algorithmic concepts in Java. Practice these problems thoroughly, understand their underlying principles, and adapt your solutions to various interview scenarios to improve your readiness for technical interviews in the field of software development.

Made in the USA
Middletown, DE
13 September 2024